SIMON PERRY

Jesus Farted

The Vulgar Truth of the Biblical Christ

First published by Thrydwulf Cambridge 2023

First edition

Narration by Dr T. Atkin

This book was professionally typeset on Reedsy.
Find out more at reedsy.com

In memory of Richard James Perry, 1972-2019

Contents

VI Concluding Reflections

I

Introduction

The Importance of Messianic Flatulence

A PORTACABIN WITH A VIEW

My tutor in ancient Greek once had in his class a student whose first language was modern Greek. The word that in Ancient Greek meant 'to break', in modern Greek, sounds like the verb 'to break wind'. Attempting to translate a well-known New Testament text out loud in class, the student effortlessly declared, 'While they were eating, Jesus farted, shared it with the disciples, and said "this is my body"' (see Mt 26:26). No Christian should find this offensive. Christians believe, after all, that Jesus of Nazareth was God 'incarnate', i.e., that in this historical figure, the CEO of the multiverse became fully and utterly and thoroughly human. To be human is to fart. If you break bread, you break wind.

Jesus farted. He pissed, he shat, he vomited, he sweated, he diarrhoea-ed, and he farted. He secreted bodily fluids and excreted bodily solids. And the intestinal perfumes he released into God's clean earth did not smell heavenly. By Christian logic, to deny this is heresy. To oppose this is blasphemy. To ignore this is idolatry. To take offence at this is apostasy. Nevertheless, throughout Christian history the most basic, bodily elements of Jesus' humanity have been concealed from view, and with drastic consequences. This book is an attempt to reveal an alternative picture of Jesus, at odds with the portrait presented by Christian religion but thoroughly compatible with that offered by the Christian Bible.

I will focus exclusively on the four 'Gospels' (Matthew, Mark, Luke and John), the opening books of the New Testament that narrate events surrounding the execution of a dangerous Jewish dissident. Unlike the overwhelming majority of historical texts, these accounts were not written nor commissioned by the victors, the elites, the learned or the power brokers. Jesus of Nazareth was a peasant builder, living alongside other peasants in peasant communities. The stories he told were designed to be memorable and memorisable, and the stories told about him were likewise both memorable and committed to memory. The communities of peasants, slaves and misfits that treasured his sayings and deeds, committed them to memory as simple stories that wasted no words but retained their power in vulgar language. And when a community chooses to remember, all manner of social safeguards are in place to preserve accuracy and reliability. Only when those communities were threatened by the Roman war machine that blitzkrieged its way through ancient Palestine a generation after Jesus' death, did it become necessary to commit these sayings to writing. (In the ancient Mediterranean world, writing was widely deemed a less reliable recording device than social memory – and for good reason). Hence, by the time the Gospels were written, the language they used had been filtered through decades of streamlining amongst the peasant communities of an agrarian society.

When these texts are studied today, their social context is rarely taken into account. Instead, Jesus is often depicted in the noble garb of a Roman emperor, issuing his teaching as dictates from on high rather than as desperate pleas from the margins. His priests, even today, sometimes dress themselves in the robes of the very authorities that silenced, tortured and killed this prophet whom they had denounced as an ideological terrorist. In reality, Jesus was deemed 'trailer trash' – the marginalised and demonised product of a feral underclass. His teachings were at first ignored, then opposed, then denounced, then finally criminalised by those who considered him a threat. Ultimately, as the centuries ground on and the groundswell of popular support for his radical policies became unstoppable, his teachings had to be re-interpreted. The dominant idea of Jesus today is the result of the brilliant imperial attempt to re-interpret and thereby re-market the radical prophetic agitator as a docile, spiritualised, non-political do-gooder.

To rediscover Jesus of Nazareth in his native vulgarity is no easy task. For the last twenty years I have asked myself over and over why this might be.

Why has neither the church nor the academy sought to make any serious effort to picture Jesus within the rough, gritty reality of the building sites where he worked as a lowly construction worker for instance? The theory I propose in this book is that those sufficiently privileged to produce academic books about Jesus of Nazareth are – for that very reason – unlikely to have much experience working on a building site, or to have been submerged in the relentless daily grind of the semi-skilled worker. This is not necessarily a failure of scholarship (we all cast historical figures in our own image to some extent), so much as it is an unavoidable but unacknowledged 'blind spot'.

My working life began as a 17-year-old care assistant in a retirement home where days were filled with the odour of incontinence and wiping butt-sludge from the reverent arses of those no longer able to reach beneath their own. The first instruction I received on the first day of my first job came from the lips of a dignified elderly First World War veteran and is forever etched into my psyche: 'Give it a good scoop!' I spent a lot of time in toilets, to the point where cleaning up defecatory mishaps became a matter of routine. From there I joined the military, teaching myself A-Levels whilst sitting in guardrooms, barrack blocks or portacabins. After seven years of military service, I had a succession of jobs as a care-worker, a security guard, a scaffolding manager, and a parker of gigantic seafaring oil-tankers. Prior to arriving at Oxford as a 'mature' 25-year-old student, I had spent an inordinate amount of time in portacabins, alongside manual labourers and low paid workers with little hope of a comfortable future. These were not just 'summer jobs' where unwittingly privileged students attend to earn pocket money. Portacabin jobs are usually worked by those who will never know any different. Before entering the world of churchly ministry and academia, my real theological formation had already taken place in these portacabins where I felt thoroughly at home. These are not the crude and unpleasant environments many people might imagine. Well, okay they probably are. But the people there are no less insightful and no more susceptible to propaganda than the intelligentsia of the gentleman's club or the Ivy League college. Nor are they any less moral or any more godless than the faithful worshippers at a lively church or serious bible-study group. Anyone who has made themselves at home in the portacabin environment already knows this. Unfortunately, very few of them find their way either into the university or the church.

I don't know how many popular books about Jesus of Nazareth have been written by those who hail from the world of the portacabin. Nor do I know how many are written by those who have never experienced poverty (except when they were a student) or hunger (except when dieting). But for sure, to those who have undergone and reflected on these experiences – the Jesus they find when studying Scripture in its historical, political, linguistic, and theological context is a full-bodied, politically engaged, radically prophetic firebrand. I suspect such people are few in number.

Most Christians simply cannot cope with the sheer humanity of the Jesus they claim to worship. The subconscious default image of the historical Jesus is an aloof character, out there and up there somewhere. A pious human-like ghostly carpenter who gently hovered his way through Ancient Israel without ever stubbing his toe, getting sawdust in his eye or hitting his thumb with a hammer. But can you even imagine praying to a deity who – at some point in his history – knew what it was to experience the build-up of intestinal gas, and to revel in the satisfaction of releasing it through his God-given rear outlet valve? Let me ask that again. Christians who cannot imagine that, are praying to the wrong deity.

The fart-less Jesus of Christian piety is, in reality, the product of a Christian heresy. Heresy itself is a post-biblical invention, designed to maintain uniformity of faith throughout a growing mass of uncontrollable and diverse believers. The fart-less Jesus is one dimension of a heresy called 'Docetism'. Based on the Greek verb 'to seem' (dokeo), Docetism is the conviction that Jesus was not really human – he only *seemed* human. Christianity is supposed to be based on the belief that in Jesus of Nazareth, God became a human being. Docetism declares instead, 'well, he didn't *quite* become human. That would be too vulgar.' In other words, Jesus was too much of a godly figure to have been mired in the real shit that real people face in real life. In the end, the 'Docetism' unwittingly adopted by so many today, thus leaves Jesus unable to fart – one of the most humane bodily functions. My claim is simply that if you cannot hear Jesus fart, you cannot hear his biblical voice.

In what follows, I will trace stories of Jesus from Mary's prenatal appointment with a senior angelic consultant, through his birth and childhood, his commissioning of twelve lieutenants, his political campaign through Galilee, the turmoil he created in Jerusalem and eventually his execution as a rebel. Every chapter is comprised of short sections, each one a literary checkpoint, narrating a brief reading from the Bible. I make no attempt to defend the plausibility of the Bible here, but simply to cite it as the authority protestant Christians in particular venerate above all else. To interpret these readings properly requires that some form of bowel movement be heard within or brought to the text.

TOILETRY WONDER

This book is not structured primarily to be read in one sitting (so to speak). Since toilet humour is best taken in small doses, the chapters below are subdivided into smaller sections that may be read as a set of brief daily reflections. The ideal location for such pondering is, of course, the toilet.

The pragmatic throne of the closet is a setting woefully undervalued as a seat of learning, and for several reasons. Firstly, it is one of the few places in the modern world in which we may find genuine peace and quiet – so long as you have not smuggled your smartphone into your solitude. The church reformer and theologian, Martin Luther (1483-1546) claims that his first epiphany from the Holy Spirit came to him whilst sitting on the latrine (a revelation from which erupted modern western civilization as we know it). That sole, private excrementary experience thus had a global impact. Secondly, those familiar with Jewish insight know there is a godly gratitude arising from a successful toilet experience – which is why there are Jewish prayers and blessings for just such an occasion. As people age, gratitude for toilet success seems to increase – a base reminder of our true status, evoking a sense of wonder at the miracle of human existence. Thirdly, modernity has promoted the myth that thinking is a purely mental exercise. It is not. We think with our mind, our heart, our stomach, our genitals, and – according to biblical tradition – (as we shall see) with our bowels. Finally, the lavatorial bowl is the ideal receptacle in which to relieve ourselves of defunct ideas, exhale the exhaust fumes of toxic ideologies, rid ourselves of mistaken worldviews, and expel long-cherished fantasies. That final flush of the tank may serve as a mechanical 'amen' of repentance, thus preparing us to re-enter the world as renewed and revitalised beings.

The role of the toilet experience in helping us to grasp our place in the universe is helpfully outlined by the philosopher, Slavoj Zizek. According to Zizek, important variations in the design of toilets native to different Western countries reveal key aspects of the worldview that prevails in those countries. He explains:

> In a traditional German toilet, the hole into which shit disappears after we flush is right at the front, so that shit is first laid out for us to sniff and inspect for traces of illness. In the typical French toilet, on the contrary, the hole is at the back, i.e. shit is supposed to disappear as quickly as possible. Finally, the American (Anglo-Saxon) toilet presents a synthesis, a mediation between these opposites: the toilet basin is full of water, so that the shit floats in it, visible, but not to be inspected... It is clear that none of these versions can be accounted for in purely utilitarian terms: each involves a certain ideological perception of how the subject should relate to excrement.

The philosopher Hegel had identified distinguishable worldviews in the triad of Germany, France and England, and Zizek concludes that these three are reflected in the toilet design of each respective country:

> [R]eflective thoroughness (German), revolutionary hastiness (French), utilitarian pragmatism (English). In political terms, this triad can be read as German conservatism, French revolutionary radicalism and English liberalism. In terms of the predominance of one sphere of social life, it is German metaphysics and poetry versus French politics and English economics. The point about toilets is that they enable us not only to discern this triad in the most intimate domain, but also to identify its underlying mechanism in the three different attitudes towards excremental

> excess: an ambiguous contemplative fascination; a wish to get rid of it as fast as possible; a pragmatic decision to treat it as ordinary and dispose of it in an appropriate way. It is easy for an academic at a round table to claim that we live in a post-ideological universe, but the moment he visits the lavatory after the heated discussion, he is again knee-deep in ideology. (Zizek: Knee-Deep, *LRB* 2004)

Absent from Zizek's reflection is the recent Japanese phenomenon of a high-performance toilet with a control panel as complex as the cockpit of a fighter jet (though presumably without the ejector seat). The control panel activates all manner of posterial technological miracles to increase cleanliness and minimise unpleasantness: automatic seat-lifting; optimal temperature settings; anti-gravity water-jets; precision-hosing; bum-drying air-blowers etc. These toilets provide the visiting anus with everything short of a prostate exam and a cappuccino, and reflect the technological worldview designed to mask our human frailty. Not surprisingly, this rest-room technology is gradually conquering the hotels of Europe and America.

Serious reflection on the toilet experience must nevertheless take us beyond Zizek's crucial insight. In addition to contemplating the customs, the habits, the attitude and outlook on which our toileteering occurs, when considering our place in history we must cast our thoughts beyond the privileges of modern Europe. Sanitation as whole is a key component in the modernisation of our world and has had a far greater impact on our worldview than we might imagine.

The fact that – for the vast majority of the time – we need invest no thought in visiting the toilet is itself an enormous privilege. For our ancestors a visit to the latrine was an event. Today, we may visit the toilet as often as we like – day or night. We enjoy uninterrupted privacy. We face little discomfort, experience little in the way of terrible odour, and face no challenges to personal hygiene. Occasionally, experiencing a toiletry mishap might provide us with a funny story – but by and large, we can take for granted that our body's need to jettison what it has processed provides us with no discernible obstacle.

Today, when all is in good working order (the plumbing of both body and house) the toilet is a minor part of life. To view it as a key to unlocking the secrets of our entire civilization may seem extreme – but that is precisely the interpretive hurdle we must overcome. The great triumph of sanitation technology has distanced us from our ancestors in ways that – precisely because of that triumph – remain largely invisible to us. Our failure to factor toilet habits into our sense of history diminishes our capacity to hear the past. Along with double-glazing, central-heating and shrink-wrapped food, modern toilets – for all their advantages – have distanced us from our world, our neighbours, our predecessors and our bodies.

Ancient Jewish theologies knew the wisdom of integrating our physical, social, political realities with our spirituality, our beliefs and our worldview. Personal hygiene was a matter of such serious concern, it naturally found its way into religious reflection. Toilets (as we understand them today) were largely non-existent in ancient Palestine. Most toilet experiences involved squatting rather than sitting, and excrement was to be transported away from human habitations. The aching quadriceps, the putrid odour, the sloppy and sticky sounds, the insanitary conditions and the difficulties of disposal were commonplace. No doubt, because this was all that most people would have known, personal and social coping mechanisms were well in place and the tasks of the toilet may have been performed without much self-consciousness. But however the populace conducted its toiletry affairs, the location of such affairs could hardly be deemed 'public *conveniences*.' The older anyone gets, the greater the potential for a simple visit to become an ominous occasion. The 'Talmud' (a magnificent source of Jewish thought, belief and law) includes a prayer and blessing from the 5th Century CE echoing this concern.

One who enters a toilet says to the angels who accompany him at all times:

'Be honoured, honourable holy ones, servants of the One on High, give honour to the God of Israel, leave me until I enter, do my will and return to you.'

Abaye said: A person should not say this, in case [the angels] abandon him and go. Instead he should say: 'Guard me, guard me, help me, help me, support me, support me, wait for me, wait for me until I enter and come out, as this is the way of humanity.'

Upon leaving, one says: 'Blessed is he... who formed humanity in wisdom, and created in him many orifices and cavities. It is revealed and known before the throne of your glory that were one of them to be ruptured or blocked, it would be impossible to survive and stand before you.' (Berakhot *60b)*

Any interpreter of such ancient texts as those of the Bible, must cup their ears towards history, and listen out for the slops, the splats, and the rectal tremors of the past.

A PHILOSOPHY OF FARTLESSNESS

How could it be that the writers and thinkers of ancient and medieval eras were more willing than their modern counterparts to ponder humanity's toiletry adventures? And how did farting thus become unmentionable?

The 'Modern' era is not as modern as many might assume, although precisely when modernity began remains a disputed matter. Although opinions vary, most would regard Rene Descartes (1596-1650) as the principal thinker who stands on the brink of the modern era. Descartes is famous for tweeting, 'I think, therefore I am' – and the context in which he made this declaration is key to understanding modernity as a whole.

Descartes feared that your experience of the whole world might be a nothing other than a gigantic illusion, a nasty trick conjured up by a malicious demon just a few minutes ago. How do you know that you – along with all your memories – were not created this morning? How do you know that the world is not just a fantasy, drilled into your mind? All that you remember, all that you love, all for which you struggle – how do you know these are not simply illusions coldly inserted by a supernatural being that's just toying with you?

As far as Descartes was concerned, you cannot be sure of anything around you. For this reason, everything has to be doubted. Absolutely everything. However, your act of doubting is your very own: no one else can do the doubting on your behalf. And because doubting requires you to think – that very process of thinking proves that you do, after all, exist! *Cogito ergo sum.* I think therefore I am.

Today, modern humans still often regard their place in the universe in Descartes' brilliant 17th Century terms. Human beings are rational animals, who think with their head-brains. But their bodies? Although it had been impossible for Descartes to doubt the existence of his own thinking-mind, it *was* possible for him to doubt that his body existed. 'Aha', he reasoned, 'that means the mind must be made of different stuff from the body.' This became known as *Cartesian* (after Descartes' Latin name, Cartesius) *Dualism* (a non-overlapping division between two things). That is, the mind and body came to be seen as two separate substances, different and distinct. Hence, the part of me that is an *I* can have an 'out of *body* experience.' Personal trainers can chant 'mind over matter' at their sweaty customers. And Keanu Reeves can messianically liberate people's minds from *The Matrix* and reunite them with their bodies. Today, you might even be forgiven for thinking that your digital online self is like an identity, an 'I', a mind that has slipped out through the back passage of your physical self and away from your body.

The upshot of all this mind/body dualism was that God (as non-physical) was separated from his creation (which was physical). Spiritual, religious, beliefs or fantasies of the mind were one thing. The material and mundane, down-to-earth reality of the body was another. And before long, what your body does is bad, a non-rational and unholy interference with the purity of the mind. Modernists often don't like to be reminded of their non-rational, unholy, physical frailties. Or of those nasty, ugly, putrid products of their own bodies. No, says the modern dualist, I think with my mind which is located somewhere within my physical brain. With my mind I can be 'objective' – but my body? My body poisons the purity of my thoughts with 'subjective' distractions. Modern culture and beliefs, self-understanding, and scientific progress all are hugely dependent on the foundations Descartes laid out in the 17th Century.

Likewise, most modern devotees, interpreters, translators and scholars of the Bible have been thoroughly shaped by the cartesian aversion to the physical in general and to faecal matter in particular. But this excretaphobia is not shared by those who wrote and those who featured in the Bible. Human beings are made in the image of God, and throughout Hebrew Scripture,

God is compelled to action on account of movement within his almighty bowels (e.g.. Isa 16:11; 63:15; Jer 31:20; cf 2 Cor. 7:15; Phil 1:8 etc). The biblical imagery of compassion towards others is rooted in the bowels. When we decide to embody compassion, our bowels are well and truly involved in the decision-making process. In the real world, fear, anger, compassion, love – all can be felt through the bowels as well as the heart. Thanks to modernity, religious and academic elites schooled in 'cartesian dualism', have excluded the language of bowels and shit from modern translations of 'holy' scripture. Here, a return to the King James/Authorized Bible of 1611 (i.e., before modernity) is more accurate, more honest, and more true-to-life than modern translations because it does not shy away from faithfully translating crude faecal and urinal words. Indeed, the King James Bible is full of shit.

In sum, the modern world that flowed out of Descartes' philosophy, had well and truly distanced the mind from the body. It followed naturally that the brain was severed from the bowels, intellect from emotion, insight from empathy. The body then becomes simply a vehicle for transporting the mind from one experience to another. That the body itself might be an essential element of your identity seems laughable to the modernist. To allow one's body any role in decision-making is often dismissed as 'being emotional'. The bowel-driven, self-giving love of God as expressed in Hebrew and Christian Scripture – is silenced. The Church, though still calling itself the body of Christ, is constipated. It preaches a God whose actions are purely rational, removed from the constraints of the bodily, removed – in other words – from the real life, day-to-day existence of real people. And the Son of God, whose own bowels got him into trouble on more than one occasion? His down-to-earth physicality, his total at-home-ness in the portacabin, his visceral anger, his painful compassion, his full-blooded real-life fear? He has been disembowelled. His innards and giblets have been carefully removed, leaving him as a gutless, lifeless, pointless icon of the spiritual realm.

If Jesus really were the Son of God, then his mind and body, his spirit and soul, his social, political, biological, psychological dimensions are inextricably bound together. If he really were the Son of God, he would surely not have refrained from flatulence. On the contrary, he would have been so at home in his human body that he may proudly have cranked out the most impressive and expressive butt-thundering, smoke-popping arse-fireworks in human history.

II

Preparing for Conflict

Under Roman rule, inhabitants of Judea, Galilee and Samaria – like those of other imperial provinces – farmed the 'milk and honey' from the land beneath their own feet, only to see it instantly taxed away to fill foreign tables and foreign purses. Communities throughout the region faced economic hardship and slow-motion societal breakdown. How could Jewish people square this experience with belief in a God who had blessed their nation? One widespread solution that took a variety different forms, was the expectation that God would anoint a liberator to smash the yoke of oppression. Different groups within Israel treasured different expectations of how this liberator, this Christ (Greek), this Messiah (Hebrew) would achieve his purposes.

THE WORD BECAME FLESH

The Bible is not the 'Word of God'. At least, not according to the Bible. Scripture never calls itself that. For John, author of the Fourth Gospel, the Word of God was not a book, but a fragile mortal being. This being was the incarnate 'logos', a Greek term that could be translated by any number of English nouns: word, action, thing, stuff, reason, logic, communication. John's idea of 'Logos' is a dynamic, eternal, personal force that animates the universe. Always unknowable, ungraspable, and unseen, the Logos nevertheless generates real-world, tangible, visible, and universal actions. This mysterious Logos would only become even vaguely comprehensible when it manifested itself in the form of a pissing, pooping, burping, farting, tiny human creature.

> *In the beginning was the Word, and the Word was with God, and the Word was God. He was in the beginning with God. All things came into being through him, and apart from him nothing came into being that has come into being. In him was life, and the life was the light of humanity. The light shines in the darkness, and the darkness has not mastered it...*
>
> *There was the true light which, on coming into the world, enlightens everyone. He was in the world, and although the world was made through him, the world did not recognise him. He came to his own [home], but his own people did not welcome him. But to everyone who did receive him, he gave the power to become children of God, to those who believe in his name, who were born, not of bloodline nor of the will*

of the flesh nor of the will of a man, but of God. And the Word became flesh, and made himself at home among us, and we saw his glory, the glory of the father's only son, full of grace and truth.
(John 1:1-5, 10-14)

An unchurched teenager in London heard the Christmas story for the first time in a Religious Studies lesson. Appreciating the story, he quietly asked the teacher at the end of the lesson, 'Why did they give the baby a swear-word for a name?' (recounted by Stuart Murray-Williams).

That teenager was probably much closer to the vulgar truth of Christmas than most theologians. The 'incarnation' is the belief that the God of heaven and earth became human: 'the Word became flesh', reason became physical, truth became mortal. For Christians who stop to think, the implications are monstrously offensive. In Jesus of Nazareth, the Director General of the cosmos squeezed his almighty personage into a tiny two-legged mammal with no bowel or bladder control. The pre-existent power holding together every atom of the universe, subjected itself to all crude human struggles, including those of the latrine. This most basic element of our shared humanity is worthy of serious reflection.

A human being's toiletry travails do not end with potty training. Nor do they begin with the cruel indignities of advancing age. Everyone, at some point in their lives will encounter some form of alien chemical intrusion that triggers demonic malpractice in one's guts. The results can render the turd cutting mechanism at the end of the back passage inoperative, either because it jams closed, causing excretal traffic to back up into your body – or because it is left open, allowing the contents of your lower intestine unrestricted access to the outside world. Two examples will suffice.

Firstly, after eating God-knows-what, by some diabolical means, your body conjures up an oversized mahogany baton. This full-sized, hard-baked, faecal baguette then cheese-grates its way down the soft tissue lining of your poo tube, confronting the turd cutter with overwhelming force. Needless to say, the human victim of such an event is reduced to a state of helpless agony. Once forced open, the cutting mechanism is disabled by the unholy mass as it passes through – a product whose front end can thereby break the surface of the waters beneath before the rear end has parted company with the host. On surviving such an experience, even the most militant atheists may find themselves automatically uttering an involuntary prayer of thanksgiving.

A second and opposite problem for mortals is the experience of one's infected gut transforming itself into a food blender that liquidizes all that has been eaten into a vegetable poop soup. My three-year old son once described this as 'a dirty poo'. On inspecting the lavatorial bowl after this watery broth has evacuated the body, it is easy to see why. Without sufficient thickness, the turd cutter has nothing to cut and transforms instead into a rectumular spray diffuser. The result is that instead of 'pissing through your arse' in a disciplined and orderly fashion, you unleash an explosive scatter splatter. Sheer carnage thus ensues, as all manner of debris pebble-dashes the pristine porcelain of your toilet bowl.

Now imagine the Eternal Logos, Commander in Chief of the Cosmos, inventor of black holes and atoms, undergoing such ordeals. At the crudest level, that is the incarnation. The creator of the thriving galaxy beyond the range of the telescope, the creator of the quark beneath the gaze of the microscope, this almighty God of space and time, subjected him or herself to filth-ridden human frailty. And, of course, did so into a world without a toilet bowl, without privacy, and without a sewage system. This is the world into which 'the word became flesh'. The emperor of the universe would be born not into a palatial estate with a Japanese toilet, but into a peasant hovel. The majestic Lord of time and space became 'trailer trash', the underprivileged outsider from the vulgar masses, crude and uncouth. That is who this Jesus is, and – according to scripture – God points at him and says, 'this is exactly who I am.'

Most Christians tend to miss the radical implications of God becoming so intolerably and disgustingly mortal. The majority assume that an all-powerful God is not so much revealed as concealed in the person of Christ. The omnipotent God, we are told, does not show himself, but disguises himself as a weak and vulnerable peasant. The monarch of heaven does not express his power, but suppresses it in order to become human. Even if –

in your Yule-tide festivities – you should 'hark' and hear what 'the herald angels sing', Jesus is not the 'Word *become* flesh', he is only '*veiled* in flesh.' The life of Jesus thus becomes an act of divine espionage, in which God pretends to be something other than he really is in order to infiltrate the ranks of humanity.

Real people can smell bullshit. And this pseudo-biblical version of Jesus secretes bullshit through every pore of his being. It is little wonder he is widely rejected. He has nothing of value to say to any except the unwittingly privileged. What right does he have to speak of experiences he has not encountered for himself? In contrast, the Jesus of the Bible was common, poor and vulgar. He was subjected not only to human frailty, but to the lower echelons of human frailty.

His contemporaries lived under the whip of a brutal empire. The majority of folk who had been longing for liberation, presumed that it would trickle down from above, the exertions of a great warrior king, from nobility or royalty or fame. But this is not the form taken by the God of scripture. Jesus was subjected to all the vulnerabilities of economic harshness faced by many of us today: food scarcity, employment insecurity, and uncertainty about whether the roof over your head or the ground under your feet would remain yours. This the setting where God made himself at home.

He was not what anyone expected. Though he fulfilled prophecies, he did so in hideously unexpected ways. He did not wield power in any conventional sense. He had no resource capital and commanded no army. The true story of Christmas is rather that the powerless, self-giving, political love embodied in this fragile Christ – is supposed to reveal an alternative power-dynamic. It is little wonder he managed to piss a lot of people off, that he defied expectation and sparked a revolution. Within a generation of his death, his name had become a term of contempt. That London teenager was onto something important – because only as we grapple with why Jesus became a swear-word, do we begin to get a true glimpse at what Christmas really is.

ZECHARIAH AND ELIZABETH

Herod the Great was an astute political leader. Even after he had allied himself with the ill-fated Mark Anthony in Rome's civil war (31BCE), Herod managed to find favour with his master's enemy, Octavian. Once Octavian had overcome all threats to his rule, he became Augustus – the first emperor of Rome. Augustus commanded Herod's loyalty, and Herod honoured his emperor by commissioning magnificent architectural projects. The crowning jewel of these was the beautiful Temple in Jerusalem. At the time of Jesus' birth, the Temple was midway through an ambitious rebuilding project, its new stone walls transformed into gleaming gold by the alchemy of searing sunlight.

In the days of King Herod of Judea, there was a priest named Zechariah... His wife was a descendant of Aaron, and her name was Elizabeth. Both of them were righteous before God, living blamelessly according to all the commandments and regulations of the Lord. But they had no children because Elizabeth was unable to conceive, and both were getting on in years.

On one occasion when he was serving as priest before God and his section was on duty, he was chosen by lot, according to the custom of the priesthood, to enter the Temple of the Lord and offer incense. Now at the time of the incense offering, the whole assembly of the people was praying outside. Then there appeared to him an angel of the Lord, standing at the right side of the altar of incense. When Zechariah saw him, he was deeply disturbed and fear overwhelmed him. But the angel

said to him, 'Do not be afraid, Zechariah, for your prayer has been heard. Your wife Elizabeth will bear you a son, and you will name him John.'
(Luke 1:5-13)

The opening scene of the Gospel narrative takes place at Jerusalem's glorious Temple. This was the meeting place of heaven and earth – it lay at the centre of the nation, and the centre of the cosmos. In Judaism, there was only one Temple and pilgrims would visit from around the nation and around the empire to attend festivals, and to be present when priests made offerings and sacrifices on their behalf. Zechariah was a humble priest living in the Judean hill country, whose priestly order had drawn lots to determine who would have the privilege of entering the Temple to burn an incense offering. Given that there were probably around seven thousand priests in Israel, the opportunity to perform this prestigious task would come around every 20-25 years. It was a once-in-a-life-time opportunity. In reality, it would have been a moment of immense pressure – since the entire nation would be focussing on the actions of this one, humble priest. In light of the events that must now unfold, it was a moment that football commentators describe as, 'squeaky bum time.'

Whilst it is easy for modern readers to roll their eyes at the pomposity of religious performances like this, it is worth trying to put yourself into the sandals of this ageing priest. By the time he made the offering he would have been a quivering bag of nerves. The cosmic hierarchy of the priestly worldview was built into the architectural structure of the Temple. Crowning a prominent hilltop, it comprised a series of ascending precincts, each higher, smaller and more exclusive than the last. Zechariah will first have entered through the Court of Gentiles, the outer precinct – accessible to anyone – the noisy and smelly area where animals were kept ready for sacrificial slaughter. From here, the priest will have moved up to the Court of Women, walking past signs that read 'No one from another nation may enter within the fence and enclosure round the temple. And whoever is caught will have himself to blame that his death ensues.' Only ritually pure Jewish men may then ascend through the tall gates of Corinthian brass and into the Court of Israelites – this was as close as any common Israelite male could come to God's holy presence. None but priests were permitted to tread any further – and as Zechariah passed through, crowds of his fellow Israelites will all have been praying about the offering he was about to make. In sight of them all, he paraded through the Court of Priests, past a gigantic stone altar and to the final steps leading up the Sanctuary itself. Zechariah, probably for the only time in his life, climbed this, the least-trodden staircase on the planet. You can almost hear the running commentary from the portacabin: 'I bet his arse is twitchin' now.' Entering beyond the view of all, the humble priest stands inside the sanctuary, at the summit of Mount Zion, the height of Israel's hierarchy, and the pinnacle of his own career. But he is not alone.

According to the narrative – as if the moment were not already tense enough – an angel suddenly appeared in front of Zechariah. At this point, the biblical text declares that the priest was 'deeply disturbed.' The Greek text has been variously translated as 'startled', 'terribly agitated', or 'troubled'. The core notion here is – however – a serious internal movement, a churning stomach – and in the underlying Hebrew – a hurricane in the bowels. The fateful experience we sometimes feel when it seems our lowermost internal organs are being whisked in a food-blender. In fact, the Hebrew literally refers to a free flowing of the guts. That is precisely what scripture expects the reader to imagine. The crude voice from the portacabin is thus not only justified, but necessary in order to arrive at an adequate interpretation of this event. The priest is so afraid his guts are in danger of escaping through his loin cloth. It was a natural reaction to fear.

For Zechariah however, if he had indeed allowed the stench of fear to billow out through his rear-exit-chute, it would have been impossible to detect. The angel was, after all, standing right next to 'the altar of incense' so any unpleasant priestly odours would have been overpowered by the sweet-smelling scents of the offering. The very presence of this altar, not to mention the importance of an 'incense offering' in the first place, demands that the issue of smell be factored into any interpretation of this event. The incense was comprised of a mix of spices, carefully prepared and burned to produce a pleasing aroma. In fact, this practice is the origin of the word 'perfume': In Latin *per* (through) *fumare* (smoke).

Why was incense burned at all? Pleasant vapours rise to God as the aromatic dimension of prayer and worship. It is a facet of liturgical practices that may be under-appreciated in the modern west, where showers and deodorants are deemed necessary and where personal hygiene is virtually a human right. In contrast, the people of ancient Palestine, frankly, would not have smelt great at the best of times. The rare experience of a powerful, sweetly scented vapour would have been glorious. God, as revealed in Hebrew Scripture, appreciated a beautiful scent since it represented the very best of what the people could offer. Farts, on the other hand, are widely perceived as an insult. As such, unpleasant smells could not be allowed to interrupt holy activities. As one Rabbi interprets ancient scripture, should flatulence interrupt a person's prayers,

> *One who was standing in prayer and passed wind waits until the odour dissipates and resumes praying. Some say: One who was standing in prayer when he felt the need to pass wind, steps back four cubits, passes wind, waits until the odour dissipates and resumes praying. And before resuming his prayer, he says: 'Master of the universe, you have formed us with many orifices and cavities; our disgrace and shame in life are clear and evident before you, as is our destiny with maggots and worms, and so we should not be judged harshly.'* (Kitzur Shulchan Aruch, 5)

The story of Zechariah ends with the angel reassuring the priest whose bowels were in the midst of a spin-cycle with the instruction, 'Do not be afraid.' He had brought good news – promising that the priest and his ageing wife will give birth to a son (John the Baptist). Unfortunately, the priest – described as 'righteous' and 'blameless' – is not fully convinced by the angel's promise. Gabriel rewards this priestly scepticism by removing Zechariah's ability to speak, at least until the time his son is born. An incident that began with his arsehole naturally opening, ended with his face-hole supernaturally closing.

THE MAGNIFICAT

The same angel who had visited Zechariah also came to Mary to announce news that she too would give birth to a son. Mary's reaction echoed that of the old priest: she was 'sore afraid' to the extent that her own bowels began to churn. Gabriel tells her not to be afraid and declares that her son would be Israel's almighty liberator. As Handel reminds us every Christmas, to her would be born 'a Saviour, which is Christ the Lord.' Once Mary had consented to this plan, the angel departed and so began the most celebrated teenage pregnancy in human history. Mary, who was probably around fourteen years of age at the time, made her way straight to Elizabeth (the two were relatives) in the distant Judean hill country. On her arrival the cousins are overcome with ecstasy, and Mary irrupts into a wrong-headed song about the great militaristic feats her son Jesus was surely destined to accomplish.

Mary said, 'My life is amplifying the Lord,
And my spirit has found joy in God my deliverer,
Because he has paid attention to the afflicted state of his slave.
Look: from now on all generations will consider me privileged,
Because the Powerful One has done great things for me and his name is Sacred.
His loving-kindness is for those who fear him from generation to generation.
He has shown great strength with his arm.
He has caused those who are magnificent in their own minds to flee.

He has dethroned those in power, and elevated those who are oppressed.

He has filled those who were hungry with good things and expelled empty-handed those who have become rich.

He has helped Israel his servant, in remembrance of his loving-kindness.

Just as he promised our ancestors, to Abraham and his descendants forever.

(Luke 1:46-55)

After testing positive for Covid-19, one of my delightful sons claimed to have 'got' one of his siblings with what he called a 'Covid fart'. The virus can indeed be spread through one's arse, since its traces have been detected on human defecatory produce. Furthermore, the act of flatulating thrusts miniature poop-leaves (micro-flakes of excremental disgust) out into the beauty of God's creation.

My son had indeed weaponized his carnal wind-tunnel into a military grade faecal leaf-blower, maliciously blasting the airborne virus towards his target. Should his victims inhale deeply from the invisible cloud of fragmented excreta, they faced the very real possibility of contracting the virus. Still, at least the culprit was wearing an ass-mask – or as we call them in Britain, 'under-pants'. Not to mention a second layer of industrial strength denim. It was thus hardly surprising that no siblings contracted the virus, as subsequent testing confirmed. The same cannot be said, however, of the spontaneous poetic outburst of the pregnant teenager. Her warmongering meme, once set to music, has been infecting western Christianity for millennia.

Mary's anthem became known as the 'Magnificat' (the first Latin word of her verse). It has been sung daily and uncritically by Christian traditions throughout history, most of whom have inhaled all too deeply from the toxic elements of her eruption. The song is comprised of two verses. The legitimate personal gratitude of the first verse is expanded into the illegitimate nationalistic hopes of the second. Interestingly, this is a pattern echoed in many national anthems throughout the English-speaking world.

Take this verse from the *Star-Spangled Banner*, celebrating the nation's divinely granted victory over evil enemies:

And where is that band who so vauntingly swore
That the havoc of war and the battle's confusion,
A home and a country, should leave us no more?
Their blood has washed out their foul footsteps' pollution.
No refuge could save the hireling and slave
From the terror of flight, or the gloom of the grave:
And the star-spangled banner in triumph doth wave,
O'er the land of the free and the home of the brave.

Or this, from *God Save the King*:

O Lord our God arise,
Scatter his enemies,
And make them fall:
Confound their politics,
Frustrate their knavish tricks,
On Thee our hopes we fix:
God save us all.

In both cases, the songs – like Mary's – appeal to a God who oversees the military defeat and shame of 'our' enemies. It is hardly surprising that ancient nations, and modern nation states, should have promoted such an ideology. Although Mary's song faithfully expressed the nationalistic hopes of her contemporaries – it was those very hopes that God would 'confuse' and 'confound'. This is certainly the story as it is expressed in Luke's Gospel. Mary, like Zechariah and his son John the Baptist, belongs to that chorus of characters who – despite being 'upright' and 'blameless' – found their own expectations subverted by Jesus of Nazareth. It is a matter of profound and tragic irony, that the bloodthirsty elements of Mary's hope that were comprehensively deconstructed by the story of Jesus as it unfolds, have been left intact and celebrated by the Christian Church. From early in Christian history, Mary's song was ripped away from its context in Luke's narrative and treasured as a stand-alone 'Canticle' i.e., a liturgical meme with a decontextualised life of its own. That is, an element of the Bible story that has been set to music and sung in churches around the globe as a celebration of the Christian story. Every church and every choir that merrily belts out this joyous affirmation of violent religious extremism thus constitutes a military grade faecal leaf-blower, with a fish badge.

By the end of the Gospel, no one has been dethroned, the oppressors remain smugly triumphant, the oppressed have not been lifted up and the hungry have not been fed. The Galilean economy was in a desperate state, land-seizures were commonplace, social banditry was on the rise, and the atmosphere was already starting to fester into a bitter turmoil that would eventually drive the country headlong into a doomed national rebellion. Within a generation, the inhabitants of Jerusalem will be so hopeless and dehumanised that they resort to cannibalism. Of course, Christians will object that the language of Mary's second verse is merely symbolic. But there is no refuge here. Try to imagine yourself back into the kind of desperate revolutionary context of first century Galilee in which Mary had learned to think, to believe, to hope and to act. People living under such circumstances are highly unlikely to trade in symbolic cries for actual liberation. Do people on the brink of starvation, living under the whip of imperial masters, really seek spiritual salvation? The claim that Mary's hopes were 'metaphorical' are delusional in the extreme. Many, many Jewish people, naturally and deeply and justifiably longed for the downfall of their oppressors. A messianic leader would be expected to precipitate that downfall.

Jesus defied expectations only because he fulfilled them so profoundly. As he embarks on his campaign, he would indeed address the revolutionary aspirations of his people. Although he would not achieve this militarily, nor could it be said that this was because he was only interested in apolitical spirituality. It was only by drawing attention to an alternative means of exerting power, an alternative means of engaging politically, and an alternative strategy for dealing with one's enemies – that the enemies of

Israel would find themselves disarmed. As will become clear in the course of the story that follows, this is the revolution Jesus would trigger. It may then – after all - be said that Mary thus spoke (or sang) more truth than she herself realised at the time. But for Mary there was no way to access this 'more truth' without first having her own expectations overturned.

The same is no less true of those who seek to belt this song out today. The overwhelming majority are unwitting victims, carriers, and spreaders of the virus that is manifests itself in war. Naturally, to regard war as a virus is an offence to a world that believes in free-will. But from the perspective of the Jesus portrayed in the Gospels, militaristic violence is a viable option only for those whose worldview has been hopelessly infected by toxic ideologies: where the nomadic god of the sky (or in Greek, 'the heavens') is reduced to an immobile god of the land (endorsing nationalism). Thus, if our land is threatened, so is our God. And if our God is threatened by pagans, then war is how he is destined to save us.

Those who waft the Magnificat from the church out into the world, thus promote a Christianity at odds with the Gospels. The musical meme leaves intact the parasite that Jesus will exorcise. It endorses the very worldview Jesus will deconstruct. It invisibly thrusts its godless ideological flatulence out into the world, all in God's name. The biblical word for this practice is 'blasphemy'.

THE BIRTH OF JESUS

Caesar Augustus – formerly known as Octavian – was the first emperor of Rome. By the time Mary and Joseph travelled to Bethlehem in accordance with imperial decree, Augustus had ruled for over two decades and was at the height of his power. The contrast is stark. The most successful dictator the world had (and arguably, has) ever seen, touches the zenith of his imperial magnificence at the very moment an unremarkable child is born in a provincial shithole. The irony is deliberate. Son of God was a Roman imperial title. Jesus – by contrast – was the son of peasants. Yet, it is precisely his vulgar status that gives him a greater claim to the title, Son of God. Gospel readers are invited to revisit their notion of a god and their notion of the kind of power a god might wield.

> *It came about that in those days a decree went out from Caesar Augustus for all the world to be registered. This was the first registration when Quirinius was governor of Syria. Everyone went to be registered, each to their own city. Joseph also went up from Galilee, from the city of Nazareth, into Judea to the city of David, which is called Bethlehem, because he was of the house and lineage of David, to be registered with Mary his betrothed who was pregnant. As it happened, while they were there, the time came for her to give birth, and she gave birth to a son, her firstborn. She wrapped him in swaddling cloths and laid him in a feeding trough, because there was no space for them in the guestroom.*
> *(Luke 2:1-7)*

The young mother arrived at full term whilst visiting a small town near Jerusalem, called Beth-Lechem (house of bread). The nativity scene is familiar to anyone who has ever received a Christmas card. According to the Christmas carols, angels, shepherds, and wise men all pitch up to witness the holy birth. According to scripture this is all pure fantasy. The Christmas scene has been sanitized in the popular imagination, to the point where a holy birth means a baby that doesn't so much as shed a tear. According to the old favourite, 'Away in a Manger', even when he is woken up by noisy cattle in the overcrowded stable, 'the little lord Jesus, no crying he makes.' (Having seen the epic movie *Ben-Hur*, I know for a fact that the little lord Jesus certainly *did* crying make.)

Nevertheless, the idealised scene continues to hold sway – so much so that this long-awaited infant is barely human. Take Pope Francis, who delivered an inspiring and heart-warming Christmas address about the smile of the baby Jesus, which included the following reflection.

> Jesus is the smile of God. He came to reveal to us the love of our Heavenly Father, His goodness, and the first way He did so was to smile at His parents, like every new-born child in this world. And they, the Virgin Mary and Saint Joseph, because of their great faith, were able to accept that message, they recognized in Jesus' smile God's mercy for them and for all those who were waiting for His coming, the coming of the Messiah, the Son of God, the King of Israel. (Pope Francis, *Christmas Greeting*, 2019)

The difficulty (and perhaps the unintended profundity) of Francis' homily, is found in the experience that every parent knows. When a baby smiles, it is not because of joy at the presence of parents. For babies, their sense of social dynamics (not to mention their eyesight) is not sufficiently developed either to recognise parents or consciously smile at them. When a baby smiles it is for one reason: profound relief from the discomfort of an internal gaseous build up. That discomfort has exited the tiny body through its God-given rear-end sluice-gate. For the first few weeks of their lives, babies smile because they experience the glory that is a liberating gust of nappy-filling diaper delight. If Jesus was a fully human baby (rather than a fake pseudo-human imposter) then yes, he did smile, and yes it was because he released wind. And here the unwitting profundity of papal insight runs deep. If Mary and Joseph recognised in the smile of their new-born infant the promise of God's saving action – they thereby had faith to recognise the wondrous significance of his world-redeeming fart.

Let me emphasize again, that this by no means trivialises the scene, but lends it historical authenticity and theological weight. The saviour's swaddling clothes will, at some point in a serious nativity scene, have been soiled. This does not reduce something sacred to crude profanity. If anything, it is quite the reverse: this is the elevation of the profane – and the Bible demands precisely this. Christmas is traditionally the Christian celebration that remembers how the God of creation, the CEO of the multiverse, became fully and properly human in order to save humanity from hoovering itself up out of existence. To become human is to be subject to the human physical condition – and that includes involuntarily introducing toxic bodily vapours into the wondrous beauty of the earth. A crucial dimension of the Christmas story is this: Jesus farted, and if he hadn't there could be no salvation for humankind.

The Gospel story portrays a God who makes himself thoroughly at home not in the courts of the king or the palaces of the emperor, but in a context of stinking poverty, in a world that has no room for him. Christmas cards today would do well to be furnished with smells, a 'scratch-n-sniff' option that would allow a fuller experience of the true meaning of Yuletide celebration.

It ought also be noted that farting does not end with infancy. The Gospels report very little about Jesus' childhood – but lists one incident where, as a 12-year-old, he had been grossly inconsiderate towards his parents. The conclusion was that Jesus modified his behaviour and returned home, where he still had a lot of growing up to do (Luke 2:52). The incident reveals very little, but offers enough of a glimpse to demonstrate that Jesus was not a miniature saint, floating flawlessly through a childhood devoid of fun, mischief and all the things that make children laugh. We must therefore assume that at some point, Jesus was a full-on human boy who – like all other children – laughed at people's farts and engaged in childish practice of performing them for amusement. At some point, kids enjoy farting and revel in the magnificence of their own greatest rectal accomplishments. Human children do this. It is grotesque in the extreme to accept for a moment the twisted morality of our beloved carol, 'Once in Royal David's city' which coldly asserts,

Christian children, all must be
Mild, obedient, good as he.

(Presumably, the hymn-writer turned a blind eye to the incident where 12-year-old Jesus forced his parents into a frantic and terrifying three-day search for him – while he sat debating the finer points of Jewish Law with teachers in the Temple.). No. Jesus was human, and that meant he was a child, and that meant that at some point in his life he was amused by farting and partook in the practice willingly. It may be sobering – and for the unwittingly heretic Christian masses it will seem blasphemous – but today it is necessary to picture the Son of God lifting his leg, rattling his cack-flaps, cranking out a minging burbler, and laughing about it. Rather than assuming that – as a divine being – Jesus did not fart, it is perhaps better to imagine that his would be the Rolls-Royce of flatula, burbling with the thunderous beauty of a Spitfire's Griffon Engine. Christians who pray to *that* Jesus are praying to someone real.

This impious demand for taking seriously the sheer, base, human reality of the Jesus worshipped by Christians is in order that Christians might have a fuller sense of what they are doing when they praise their saviour. Listening out for Jesus' world-transforming fart might then result in a genuine, God-given and life-giving smile.

JOHN THE BAPTIST

John the Baptist was the latest in a line of popular resistance figures in Jewish history. He had amassed an enormous following, countless Israelites who had come to the River Jordan to re-enact a crucial element of their ancestral legacy. Many centuries earlier, a confederacy of Jewish tribes had crossed this river to take possession of the land. By returning to emerge again from the waters of the Jordan – John's followers were claiming to be a new Israel. Naturally, this brought John to the jealous attention of those who safeguarded the traditions of the old Israel.

The beginning of the good news about Jesus the Messiah, the Son of God, as it stands written in Isaiah the prophet:

I will send my messenger ahead of you, who will prepare your way— a voice of one calling in the wilderness, 'Prepare the way for the Lord, make straight paths for him.'

So John the Baptist appeared in the wilderness, announcing a baptism of repentance for the forgiveness of sins. The whole Judean countryside and all the people of Jerusalem were going out to him. Confessing their sins, they were being baptized by him in the River Jordan. John was clothed with camel's hair and a leather belt around his waist. He is easting locusts and wild honey. And he was campaigning, saying, 'After me comes the one more powerful than I, the straps of whose sandals I am not worthy to stoop down and untie. I baptize you in water, but he will baptize you in the Holy Spirit.'

(Mark 1:1-8)

For a few months in 1994 I undertook casual employment at Marine Port Services as part of a crew that parked gigantic oil tankers in the Milford Haven estuary and hooked them up to pump liquid gold into the refineries. (This was long before I realised that working for an oil company warrants an eternity in hades). The job involved being called out at short notice, any time of day or night and then spending hours on end waiting in a portacabin for a ship that – fingers crossed – may not arrive until after our shift had finished. This meant, in turn, a diet of fast-food, unhealthy snacks and hurriedly prepared packed lunches. One crew member, however, was too health-conscious for such a diet. Georgie proudly boasted that he had recently switched exclusively to eating beans and peas which he claimed allowed him all the protein, nutrients and fibre his body needed. (I was too shy to ask how his 2-litre bottle of diet lemonade fitted into the regime).

One morning, some time around 2-3am, an impromptu flatulence tournament began. Multiple ani released their fumes into a devastating gaseous cocktail. The atmosphere quickly became putrid and the sound was positively demonic. I recall feeling asphyxiated in that chamber of horrors and that my sentence in hades had already commenced. The worst was yet to come. Georgie opened his legs and generated an ear-splitting sphincteral rumble of cavernous plenty, unceasing in duration, and accompanied by the triumphant grin of an Olympic champion. But as the rest of the portacabin was already collapsing into laughter, his face suddenly changed. In a fleeting nano-fragment of time, Georgie's proud smirk was displaced by an expression of sheer horror.

Yes.

He had been pushing so hard, he experienced what might be deemed 'nuclear fallout'. His fears were confirmed by the muffled squelch and the rancid stench now billowing out from the welsh fudge lodged inside his overalls. This proved too much for Barry, one of the other crew members, who was already doubled up in uncontrollable laughter. A dark patch quickly spread from the groin area of Barry's orange overalls. He had surrendered bladder-control. Through the cacophony of hysterical howling that followed, I heard someone hyperventilate, 'that's two for the price of one.' It's a phrase that still makes me snigger. But reading about John the Baptist also reminds me of Georgie's unfeasible mishap.

The diet of John the Baptist was not dissimilar to that of Georgie. It is possible that he literally gobbled up 'locusts and wild honey', but more likely that 'locust' here refers to the 'locust bean' which sprouts from a shrub that was native to the Eastern Mediterranean region. Since these beans are members of the 'legume' family, their effects on the human body are what you might expect. Containing galacto-oligosaccharides (which are non-digestible) they foment in the gut causing bloating and flatulence. The saintly version of the Baptist, robed in dazzling white raiment and conducting a pious procedure designed to instil ritual purity is quite mythical. The original Baptist, after all, clothed himself in camel hair – coarse, uncomfortable and smelly. The practice of baptism today, even when performed on adults, tends to endorse the sanitized notion of purity, whiteness, perfection – all representing an image of pristine moral life that qualifies pious Christians to spend all eternity living inside a shampoo commercial. A moment's reflection on the diet, the clothing and the angry demeanour of John reveals that baptism in the Gospel story has little in common with contemporary practice in most church traditions.

In all likelihood, baptism itself involved those who were being baptised wading out waist-deep into the Jordan river, before John plunged (the literal meaning of 'baptise') the rest of their bodies beneath the surface. This had little to do with symbolically washing people clean. It was a 'prophetic action.' Prophets, in Jewish tradition, were not merely people who predicted the future – so much as those who spoke truth to power. Usually, they would do this in protest to corrupt leadership in their own day – and often they used not only written and spoken words, but vivid, physical symbolism. These dramatic, symbolic actions include marrying a prostitute, smashing pots, wearing an ox's yoke, and shaving one's own head. Submerging Israelites beneath the waters of the Jordan was, above all, a prophetic act of this nature. What did it signify?

That the nation as a whole was soon to undergo catastrophic judgement. Just as an individual was plunged beneath the waters and re-emerged to a different life – so would the nation as a whole be submerged under the fire of unspeakable disaster. Historically, this happened a generation later, when the Roman war machine ground its way through Galilee and Judea. The Temple would be destroyed, and the people humiliated and displaced. For the nation of Israel, life as they knew it had come to an end – and a radically different, post-traumatic existence began to develop. The symbolism of baptism was thus, 'the status quo you treasure is a fantasy that will soon collapse. Best you get yourself ready.' How?

The text describes John's activities as a 'baptism of repentance for the forgiveness of sins'. Today, we regard 'repentance' as some spiritual transaction designed to 'clear history' of one's dubious activities, wiping clean our moral hard drive before a cold and calculating divinity obsessed with punishing people. Repentance is something else. It refers to a fundamental transformation of worldview, a 'paradigm shift'. The glib and shallow virtue of open-mindedness is a self-congratulatory delusion by comparison. To change one's mind about anything that actually matters is a traumatic experience – it subjects your entire being to ideological upheaval. The Greek word for repentance is 'metanoia' – meta (after), nous (mind). To displace one mindset with another is a near impossible feat, which is why John symbolised it with the dramatic act of baptism. But what does this have to do with sin?

'Forgiveness of sin' is a phrase whose root meaning is economic. In the original language, 'forgiveness' means liberty and 'sin' means debt. In an empire that depended on every citizen and slave honouring their debts – forgiveness of sin (i.e., debt cancellation) is a dangerous political and economic threat. For those who were submerged beneath the Jordan River – their debts were consigned to a watery grave. When they re-surface, people are declared debt-free, before their fellow Israelites, before their leaders, and before their God.

All these elements of baptism as explained in the Gospels have been conveniently ignored by the staggering majority of Christians throughout history. Where baptism had been the *rejection* of a delusional status quo, most – especially those baptised as infants – have undergone baptism in order to *conform* to a Christianised status quo. A Christianised worldview whose morality is based on *honouring* debt instead of *forgiving* it. In the digestive tract of a Christianised worldview, baptism has thus been processed into its own exact opposite. What would John the Baptist make of this twofold re-interpretation of baptism? Where baptism today is all-too-often the gateway to compliance rather than resistance, and to debt-subjugation rather than debt-amnesty? The historian in me can hear John snigger, 'That's two for the price of one.'

THE BAPTISM OF JESUS

Jesus' first proper appearance in the Gospel narrative is as a man of around thirty years of age. No followers. No reputation. He was simply a builder from an obscure village in Lower Galilee, a region surrounded by pagans and a hotbed of political rebellion.

> *Then Jesus came from Galilee to the Jordan to be baptized by John. John attempted to deter him, saying, 'I need to be baptized by you, and do you come to me?' Jesus replied, 'Make it so! It is necessary for us to do this to satisfy the demands of justice.' Then John consented. As soon as Jesus was baptized, he came up out of the water. Instantly the sky was opened, and he saw the Spirit of God descending like a dove and resting on him. A voice from heaven said, 'This is my Son, whom I love; with him I am well pleased.'*
> *(Matthew 3:13-17)*

John the Baptist's life work had been to prepare for the arrival of God's Messiah. How was he going to react when he encountered Jesus? These two men were no anaemic, saintly, two-dimensional pawns, expressionless and lifeless, greeting one another as automated mechanical instruments in the unfolding of God's plan. They were real people, facing one another down in all their full-blooded humanity. The existence of John the Baptist is very well attested by sources external to the Bible. He triggered a significant and potentially dangerous movement in Israel, with swathes of followers faithfully devoted to him. At this early stage, Jesus did not have a single follower – and arrived at the Jordan alone, with no credentials but himself. John instantly and unquestioningly recognised and acknowledged him. You can almost hear the gravitas and anxiety of this momentous encounter in the Baptist's voice. And of course, if he was in the river at the time, then it is perfectly possible that the bean-filled-baptist momentarily transformed the Jordan into a jacuzzi. His entire life had been structured around this meeting.

The baptism of Jesus has left Christian thinkers scratching their heads for two thousand years. Because baptism has been deemed a ritual demonstration of repentance from *sin,* why on earth would a *sinless* Jesus need to be baptized at all? If there was nothing to forgive, why seek forgiveness? Was the truth that Jesus had, in fact, sinned? (In which case, the Christian story is over before it began). Or was he faking his repentance? (In which case it was just a show-baptism, devoid of real meaning). The question itself highlights the absurd reasoning into which the church was forced once it had re-branded baptism as a ritual-performance carefully severed from its prophetic origins.

As I showed in the previous section, John the Baptist was a prophet and baptism was a powerful, dramatic, symbolic, prophetic act. Israel as a whole was about to enter a new phase of its history – to undergo a baptism of fire, to experience a death and rebirth. The Temple would be destroyed, and the nation scattered. Everyone who went to be baptised became a personal, living, manifestation of what was due to take place – a microcosm of death and resurrection. When Jesus arrived, however, he was not simply another Israelite. The biblical text makes this clear by describing him as 'the Son of God'. No one present would have understood this as meaning that Jesus was the second person of the Trinity, the actual physical offspring of Israel's revered deity. This phrase had multiple meanings in the ancient Mediterranean world: the 'Son of God' was a title for the emperor; it was a label for a holy man; it was a name for Israel as a whole. It is most likely in this last sense that people would have understood the phrase. Jesus was deemed to be Israel-in-person, a figurehead for his people. It is as the representative of the nation that Jesus was baptised. His own body represented his nation in the fullest possible way. As the waters closed over him, an old chapter of Israel's story closed. As he re-emerged, so began a new era of Israel's history.

The voice out of the sky declared, 'This is my son, whom I love.' Again, the physicality of the event has to be fully appreciated before the symbolism has any validity. The notion of the *symbol* (different from a *sign* which is simply a pointer), is Greek in origin and refers to two things which are 'thrown' (*ballo*) 'together' (*syn*). It is best understood as a token, such as a coin – that is cut in half, complete only when the two pieces are fitted together. Baptism is a symbol – in which the base, brief, crude, physicality of a human action is re-connected with transcendence, otherness, eternity. When the Son of God, the figurehead of all Israel, is physically plunged beneath the waters of the Jordan – it is an event of cosmic magnitude. Whoever has unzipped the sky and spoken from heaven, is a god whose beloved offspring is no glorious emperor, pious king or beautiful priest. This is just a bloke, stood in an insignificant little river, being ducked beneath its surface by a strange figure with a sharp tongue, an odd diet, and a camel fur jacket.

This is the Jesus to whom God himself has publicly declared his own love – but whether it is the same Jesus beloved by Christians throughout space and time is another question. Most depictions of Jesus – in literature, art and film, have enabled a sugar-sweet non-human Christ figure to congeal in the popular mindset. Depictions are like travel literature – maybe hinting towards some aspects of a place that might be of interest, mark it out as different, as 'other' – a place so different it is worth visiting. Rarely do they focus on the mundane, the everydayness and everywhereness of a place, that makes it just another version of here, just another brand of familiarity. The result of much literature that seeks to teleport us to the historical Jesus, is that the mundane is omitted. The outrageously benign preacher, a Hollywood glimpse of the character with a cool soundtrack that drowns out his real voice, a messianic James Bond – no longer really 'one of us' in any real sense. When this kind of figure is venerated, worshipped and loved, the love quickly becomes dysfunctional. Christians project onto him their own ideas of holiness, godliness, goodness, and denounce anything that undermines their liturgical fantasy. The Jesus whom God loved is an actual real-life person. The Jesus loved by the Church is all-too-easily sanctified away from real-life.

I end this reflection with reference to the insights of an 18th Century clergyman who understood well enough the incapacity to accept that those we adore might be fully human. In 1734, the Very Rev'd Jonathan Swift (Dean of St Patrick's Cathedral, Dublin and author of the famous *Gulliver's Travels*) wrote *Cassinus and Peter: A Tragic Elegy*. The poem recounts two Cambridge students – one of whom has fallen profoundly in love with his sweetheart, Celia. Cassinus, however, has stumbled upon a terrible revelation about his lover that has undermined his entire worldview and left him distraught. In seeking to ascertain what crime Celia had committed, Peter is sworn to secrecy before Cassinus finally declares:

Now bend thine ear, since out it must;
But, when thou seest me laid in dust,
The secret thou shalt ne'er impart,
Not to the nymph that keeps thy heart;
(How would her virgin soul bemoan
A crime to all her sex unknown!)
Nor whisper to the tattling reeds
The blackest of all female deeds;
...
Nor to the chattering feather'd race
Discover Celia's foul disgrace.
But, if you fail, my spectre dread,
Attending nightly round your bed -
And yet I dare confide in you;
So take my secret, and adieu:
Nor wonder how I lost my wits:
Oh! Celia, Celia, Celia shits.

That realisation is the end of fantasy and the beginning of love. The transition from fantasy to love is called 'repentance,' the weight of such a shift is called 'baptism', and the near impossibility of bringing it about is called 'death and resurrection'. The proximal cause of this glorious liberation? Shit!

THE DEVIL PUTS JESUS TO THE TEST

The devil is a curious figure in the New Testament. He may be a personification of evil, so that people can give malevolence a personal name and project their loathing, frustration, revulsion and fear onto an imaginary cosmic scapegoat – the divine author of all their misfortune. Conversely, the great evils in the world may be a manifestation of some great invisible, supernatural figure with his own independent existence. Which came first: human projection or otherworldly fiend? It's only a question of chicken or egg. Fresh from his baptism and a subsequent fast, Jesus engages in extended political negotiation with this supernatural/imaginary figure variously known as the devil, Satan or Beelzebub.

Jesus was led up by the Spirit into the wilderness to be tested by the devil. After he had fasted for forty days and forty nights, he became hungry. And the devil came and said to him, 'Since You are the Son of God, command that these stones become bread.' But he answered and said, 'It is written: "You cannot live only on bread, but on everything that comes out of the mouth of God."'

Then the devil transported him into the holy city and had him stand on the pinnacle of the Temple, and he said to him, 'Since you are the Son of God, throw yourself down; for it is written, "He will give His angels orders concerning you" and "They will lift you up, so that You do not smash Your leg against a stone."' Jesus said to him, 'On the other hand, it is written: "You shall not put the Lord your God to the test."'

Again, the devil transported him to a very high mountain and showed him all the kingdoms of the world and their glory; and he said to him, 'All these things I will give You, if you take a knee and pay homage to me.' Then Jesus said to him, 'Piss off, Satan! For it is written: 'You shall worship the Lord your God, and serve only him.''' Then the devil left. And look: angels came and took care of him.
(Mt 4:1-11)

Martin Luther (1483-1546), the defiant German theologian and Reformer, offered magnificent advice on resisting the temptations of the devil.

> I am of a different mind ten times in the course of a day. But I resist the devil, and often it is with a fart that I chase him away. When he tempts me with silly sins I say, 'Devil, yesterday I broke wind too. Have you written it down on your list?' (*Luther's Works, AE 54:16*)

Unfortunately, the so called 'temptation story' is nothing of the sort. Far from trying to 'tempt' Jesus with 'silly sins', the devil 'tests' him in the way that anyone would test equipment they want to use – and Jesus failed the test in a spectacular fashion. Nevertheless, Luther's advice on using holy flatulence to withstand a satanic onslaught may still prove itself worthy. Testing, of course, is the means by which one can establish whether things or people are 'fit for purpose'. Since everyone treasured different expectations of what a Messiah's purpose would be, and how he would accomplish that purpose, the devil himself is no exception. He tests Jesus, hoping to recruit him for his own diabolical ends.

The interaction between Jesus and the devil is best understood within the context of 'patron-client' relationships – economic arrangements that enabled the Roman Empire to function. A wealthy or powerful 'patron' or 'lord' would command the loyalty of those who were useful to him for some purpose or other. A client, on the other hand, would pledge his loyalty to a superior, whose authority he would recognise and whose protection he would enjoy – in return for whatever service the client might be able to offer. The client was expected to pay homage to his patron on a regular basis. The so-called 'temptation' story is in reality, the devil's attempt to recruit Jesus as his client. As such, he recognises the legitimate goals of Jesus' messianic campaign and suggests ways in which he can help Jesus achieve those goals.

The first test concerns providing food for the dissatisfied and hungry masses who Jesus represented. Such provision would, after all, be a noble and godly priority. But Jesus points out that this is not enough – and that God expects more for them. 'You cannot live only on bread…' A messianic campaign must have a wider impact than simply 'feeding the poor,' but going beyond that has often been considered a threat to those in power. As the Brazilian archbishop, Helder Camara, is reported to have said, 'When I give food to the poor, they call me a saint. When I ask why they are poor, they call me a communist.' Should those trapped in poverty today expect any more from an unjust economic system than mere subsistence? If they do, the extreme centrists of western politics consent to the devil's limited programme. Paying their homage to major banks and pledging their loyalty to corporate sponsors, they fart in the faces of the 'huddled masses yearning to breathe free,' demonising them as a 'basket of deplorables' and 'peasants with pitchforks.' (I'll come back to those phrases later on). Jesus is one such deplorable peasant.

The second test concerns irresponsible action in the present (leaping from the Temple) on the strength of fantasy deliverance (divine salvation) in the future. The perfect example was the 'false prophet' in the last days of the Israel's glorious Second Temple, when Jerusalem and its Temple were besieged by the unstoppable legions of Rome. According to the Jewish contemporary, Josephus, this false prophet told these besieged Jews that they need not flee nor surrender to the rampaging Romans because God would supernaturally deliver them (see *Wars*, 6.5.2). Many of them leapt from the heights of the Temple and died as they landed. Again, the extreme centrists of modern-day rational liberalism behave precisely as the devil counsels. For instance, from an economic perspective, embracing 'incremental' change – in flat out *irresponsible* ignorance of all evidence to the contrary – is heralded as a sensible means of resisting the rapidly accelerating economic deterioration that beleaguers the planet. In reality incremental salvation is a *fantasy*, carefully promoted to allow economic injustice to flourish unhindered in the present. Or from an ecological perspective, investing hope for the future in some as-yet-undiscovered technological breakthrough is an *irresponsible* faith in a *fantasy*. It allows us to continue burning fossil fuels with delusional self-assuredness. Modern liberals may not believe in the devil, but merrily adopt the fairy tale hopes he continues to sell them. They may as well leap from the heights of the Temple.

The third test concerns power. The devil urges Jesus to survey the kingdoms of the world – taking these as legitimate models for exercising power, and a potential source of his own power as Messiah. All Jesus need do to access this power, is to pay homage to the devil. Of course, the process of paying homage puts you in the service of power-brokers – not in the service of those whom God has prioritised (i.e, those stricken with poverty). This has been a pattern in Christian history that is repeated in contemporary secular liberalism. In the fourth century, the church sought to fulfil its mission to the poor, by accessing the secular powers of the Roman empire – and some clergy in Anglican and Catholic tradition continue today to wear the robes of Roman senators from this era. This clothing itself suggests that – unlike Jesus – the church passed the devil's test with flying colours (black, pure white, and costly purple in particular). The same dynamic of paying homage to those in power, in order to use that power for good, is also evident in the British Labour Party, and the US Democrat party – both of whom opted to begin accepting donations from corporate wealth in the 1990s. Again, the results were the abandonment of the working-class roots of their movements, the shift towards policies that reflect instead the interest of corporate sponsors, and the bland moralities of radical centrism that enable devotees to accept all this without vomiting.

Jesus was not so easily patronised as the figureheads of the early church or the puppet-kings of late-stage capitalism. Well-meaning but gullible leaders have always sought to utilise unjust power to serve their own pious ends. Often, all they need do is to pay homage to the true power-brokers.

Naturally, the very process of accessing this power in this way, gradually and invisibly corrupts those who succeed.

How then should we apply Luther's insight of chasing away such 'temptation' with holy flatulence?

Perhaps the beginning of an answer is found in the example of the Earl who went to pay his homage, prostrating himself before the Queen Elizabeth I. In Tudor times, Edward de Vere (1550-1604) entered the court of England's great monarch, clearly overawed by the majesty and formality of the setting. John Aubrey's 1693 account reports that, 'this Earl of Oxford, making of his low obeisance to Queen Elizabeth, happened to let a fart, at which he was so abashed and ashamed that he went to travel [for] seven years. On his return the Queen welcomed him home, and said, "My Lord, I had forgot the fart"'.

The patron-client relationship entails clients prostrating themselves before their patrons. Jesus refused. Thankfully, if we mortals are tempted to prostrate ourselves, the Creator of the human race has installed built-in a human alarm system, designed to alert us to the true nature of such actions: Today, anyone prostrating themselves (or making 'low obeisance') without engaging core, is likely to squeeze pockets of intestinal vapour out through their arse. It may be taken as nature's way of jolting us from our ethical slumber. Should we find ourselves paying homage to those with power – we would do well to allow our own body to sound its alarm. Always listen to the voice of your own arse. If the devil tempts you thusly, then – as Luther recommends – it is with a fart that we may chase him away.

III

The Galilean Campaign

Jesus began his campaign in Lower Galilee, a region with a volatile history and a revolutionary reputation. Far from the power centre of Jerusalem, its history had taken a very different course to that of Judah in the South. Judeans often sneered at folk from northern territory, describing it as 'Galilee of the Gentiles' (see Isaiah 9:1), a region polluted by paganism but that became Jesus' principal theatre of operations.

REPENT AND BELIEVE

Jesus' cousin, John the Baptist, had gained an enormous following as a people's prophet. Having denounced Herod Antipas, the puppet King of the northern territories, John was arrested and jailed, never to be released. It was at this moment Jesus entered the public arena.

> *Now after John was taken into custody, Jesus came into Galilee, delivering the good news about God, and saying, 'The countdown is complete. The reign of God is at hand. Repent and believe in the good news.'*
>
> *(Mark 1:14-15)*

In the late 60s of the first century, the aristocratic historian, Flavius Josephus, found himself reluctantly commissioned as an officer in the doomed Jewish resistance against almighty Rome. Part of his task was to unite to Jerusalem's cause the various rebel factions in the northern Galilean territory. He thus appealed to one leader with the following words: 'change your allegiance, and pledge your loyalty to me'. This is my translation of Josephus' Greek text, but when these very same words appear in the bible they are translated, 'repent' and 'believe in me'.

Words like 'repent' and 'believe' – along with the others translated above (kingdom, gospel, etc) were simply *not* religious words in the first century. To repent here, is to change your allegiance, that is – your commitment to a person, a cause, or a course of action. In a highly charged political context, it is likely to be a painful and life-changing re-alignment of your loyalties. It carries an urgency, a radical decision that cannot be taken by increments – but is all-embracing and absolute.

Repenting well is a deeply disturbing if not terrifying prospect which in practice is very much like soiling yourself in fear. That is, assuming the correctness of those who argue that shitting your pants is an evolutionary defence mechanism. The idea is that crapping oneself enables the terrified prey to reduce their bodyweight and increase their chance to escape their predator (or at least, put them off their food). The scientific veracity of this may be confirmed by the technical term for an involuntary faecal trouser-filling. The biological description for a fear-triggered defecation is 'shitting bricks' which in time morphed into the phrase, 'bricking it,' which later reverted to 'shitting it'. Hence in its origin, the phrase originally denotes the astonishing density of faecal mass your body can – through fear – jettison without your consent.

Personally speaking, if I were a cave-dwelling Englishman from prehistoric Covent Garden, were I to find myself fleeing an ambush of sabre-tooth tigers, I am not sure how helpful the sudden urge to evacuate my bowels might prove. Having to stop somewhere on Russel Square, unfasten my bear-skin diaper, and squat behind a tree would simply afford my feline predators all the time they need to decant their Bordeaux and unfold their serviettes. I would surely be left to watch the rest of my tribe disappear over the horizon to the safety of North Islington while I wipe my Neolithic ass, wash my hands, curse Charles Darwin and pray that in some distant future, my unearthed bones might feature in a documentary in which Sir David Attenborough announces to my descendants that I had given my life as a ransom for many.

In Jesus' context as in ours, to repent is firstly to confront head on the sheer urgency of the world-ending crisis we face. (It is in that prior readiness to see the world as it really is that any real decision is made). From my new position of a disturbingly corrected worldview, to 'repent' then means to jettison (almost involuntarily) my toxic ideas, misplaced commitments, comfortable ignorance, not to mention my manufactured consent to the necrophilic practices of relentless profiteering. The change of allegiance is all-encompassing.

In an age as ideologized as any, our actual allegiance is usually pledged (already and unwittingly) to the titans of corporate power. In biblical terms, that allegiance is best described as loyalty/faith/belief (all the same word in the vulgar Greek of the New Testament). In old English, belief simply meant 'by life'. In this light, I don't get to choose what I believe. The idea is rather that other people see my life and can tell from the way I live what is really important to me. However Christian or Atheist I might claim to be, the real question about my belief today is whether I live in accordance with the moral authority planted into my psyche by today's titanic powers. We live, after all, in what may well prove the last century of our species. The ecological disaster (at least, for humans) that gathers on the horizon demands urgent attention. The economic conventions (that favour profit over people) promote beliefs designed to mask this truth for as long as possible. In the face of our collective destruction, how do we respond? Here are some examples of the beliefs modern liberals unconsciously treasure:

There is no alternative (which roughly translated, means, 'I am too greedy, scared, comfortable or lazy to consider alternatives seriously').

What you see is all there is ('The echo-chamber I smugly pretend not to inhabit, tells me all I need to know').

People have to pay their debts ('Blood-stained wealth has to continue being sucked out of the planet until only the corporate vampires survive').

We need incremental change ('I want to appear as a moral crusader, whilst not giving an actual shit about real people who suffer for real here and now).

As the human race accelerates towards an irreversible state of self-destruct, the last of these creedal beliefs is perhaps the most pernicious. The desire for 'incremental change' can create the impression that we have an active, pragmatic, adequate response to the global emergency we face. It has an aura of wisdom around it since most great justice movements in history have achieved their goals incrementally. It is a fantasy, of course. Take the civil rights movement in the US. Countless courageous individuals have hurled their lives against a profit-making death-machine that is powered by the cut-price lives of slaves and their descendants. Change came only gradually as – by gargantuan acts of self-sacrifice – an unstoppable line of nameless heroic individuals prized concession after concession out of an iron-fisted, tight-fisted authoritarian regime. The fact that battles are still fought in order to edge slowly towards a fairer world, moving only by increments that are tectonically slow? Those increments would never have been gained at all unless activists devoted their entire lives to their cause. To conclude that 'incremental change' is therefore desirable (a goal rather than a consequence), is to side with the status quo of profit-hungry necro-politics.

This is true at both global and individual levels. The link between the political and the personal dimensions of 'incremental change' is not hard to trace. Lee Camp, for instance, highlights how one global investment bank report openly declares that a 'one off' act of healing a person from a terrible disease is undesirable because it is unprofitable. Camp cites the report directly:

> *The potential to deliver 'one-shot cures' is one of the most attractive aspects of gene therapy... However, such treatments offer a very different outlook with regard to recurring revenue versus chronic therapies... While this proposition carries tremendous value for patients and society, it could represent a challenge for genome medicine developers looking for sustained cash flow* (cited by Camp, *Bullet Points and Punch Lines*, 2020, 88).

In other words – at an individual level – human survival is not profitable. Administering drugs regularly (incrementally), on the other hand, enables profiteering to continue unabated. That we live in a world where such a concern is even thinkable – not to mention printable – shows the necessity of a radical shift in our worldview. As Camp concludes, 'This is a system built on the exploitation of others for gain... and that's why we need a revolution of the mind' (Camp 2020, 92). That 'revolution of the mind' (*metanoia*, in Ancient Greek) is precisely what every Jewish prophet, Jesus included, meant when they said, 'repent!'

Incremental change is the half-assed version of repentance. Given the current state of our planet, we need excremental rather than incremental change. We have swallowed whole the toxic dictates of corporate titanism and drunk deep from the well of neoliberal creeds. Individually and collectively, humanity has allowed itself to be force-fed on elitist faeces. Any healthy body would shit all of this poisonous indoctrination straight out of its carnal garbage chute – not in steady increments, but in one gloriously full-blown, one-off, one-shot excremental blow-out. If we could hear Jesus well, we would all be bricking it. Repentance is excremental change.

THE NAZARETH MANIFESTO

Jesus' message of repentance was no less revolutionary than that of his cousin, John. But unlike John (who remained planted in one location), Jesus moved around the Galilean region. His initial base of operations was the coastal town of Capernaum, but soon he would return to his home village, the place where he was guaranteed a warm reception.

> *He came to Nazareth where he had been brought up and, as usual on the Sabbath, he entered the synagogue and stood up to read. The scroll of the prophet Isaiah was handed to him, he unrolled the scroll and found the place where it was written,*
>
> *'The Spirit of the Lord is upon me, because he has anointed me.*
> *It is to bring good news to the poor that he has commissioned me:*
> *to proclaim liberation to captives and recovery of sight to the blind,*
> *to dismiss the oppressed in liberty,*
> *to proclaim the year of the Lord's favour...'*
>
> *He rolled up the scroll, gave it back to the attendant and sat down. The eyes of everyone in the synagogue were riveted to him. (Luke 4: 16-20)*

Rev Lewis Misselbrook was a former WW2 fighter pilot and the ultimate Baptist. Misselbrook had, after all, converted to Christianity underwater (in the Adriatic Sea – freshly relieved of his twin-prop Mosquito night-fighter, courtesy of a Flugzeugabwehrkanone 38 shell). Returned from the war and newly qualified as a Baptist minister he soon filled his first church with townsfolk who were curious to hear him speak. A well-meaning church elder, delighted with burgeoning congregation, whispered to Lewis, 'these are just the kind of people we want in our church.' Lewis' response was a summary of his character and his career: 'And who are the people we *don't* want in our church?' It was to those people he devoted his life. He was following in the footsteps laid out in Jesus' Nazareth Manifesto.

In his home village of Nazareth, Jesus had entered the synagogue. Nothing at all like a modern church or synagogue – the synagogues of Galilee in Jesus day were closer to debating chambers and town hall meetings. There was no sole, authorized preacher perched safely up in a pulpit six feet above criticism. Instead, speakers would take the floor and argue passionately with one another as they wrestled with the Hebrew Scriptures. When Jesus addressed those gathered, he was articulate in his manner but wildly offensive in content. He selected a text that emphasized God's allegiance with the impoverished, the outcast, the foreigner, the outsider. Furthermore, he claimed that he himself had been anointed by Israel's God to bring liberation to these people, i.e., 'the people we don't want.' These were to be the people who followed Jesus in their droves.

Saint Paul had a magnificent description for these people. He called them 'the shit of the earth' (I Cor 4:13) and regarded himself as the shittiest of their number (I Tim 1:15). Paul's words here are usually translated over-politely by a phrase that has entered popular use, 'the *scum* of the earth.' This does not do justice to the strength of Paul's conviction. The earliest followers of Christ were human excreta, the moral refuse of a strict religious code, the social turds of a respectable culture, the faecal product of an unjust economic system, the exhaust fumes of the imperial machine. And Jesus was *their* Messiah. He made himself thoroughly at home with precisely these folk. It is hardly surprising that he was beshitten, not only by the ruling elites of distant Jerusalem, but by the fellow members of his humble village.

When they heard Jesus declare that Israel's God had commissioned him to effect liberation for 'the shit of the earth', they were incensed. They grabbed hold of him and dragged him up to the top of the hill where the town was situated. Not only did they throw him out of the settlement – but they went to throw him off the hill. Some biblical scholars take this to mean that they attempted to execute him. Just as likely however, is that – in accordance with Jewish Law – the outsider is to be expelled from the company of faithful Israelites, in order to keep them holy.

In the same breath, just as foreigners and unclean Israelites are to be expelled (Dt 23:1-11) so is shit (Dt 23:12-15). Outsiders, in other words, expelled from the camp are thereby treated like shit. And to good, faithful, law-abiding religious folk, Jesus too is thus treated like shit. This was his PR launch, his manifesto pledge, the foundation for his entire campaign – and it resulted in his fellow townsfolk trying to shovel him out of the town like a moist turd.

Outsider status is becoming ever more desirable in a postmodern culture that treasures so-called free-thinking, that values the ethical rebel, the heroic misfit. Mass advertisers feed off and feed into the myth: 'dare to be different'; 'defy convention'; 'think outside the box'. These are mere manifestations of a collective delusion, statements of compliance with manufactured dissent, unwitting conformity to what some have deemed 'capitalist realism'. Historically, non-conformity was genuinely dangerous – and was practiced by those with little self-consciousness of the label, since they were driven by greater concerns than public perception. Now that non-conformity has been commodified, it is cost-free. Outsider status is enviable and attractive. It can be achieved by those who have never been hungry because they could afford no food, have never worried about whether their family will still have a home next week, have never had to hide from debt collectors. Today, anyone can select any basic human experience as a qualification for 'outsider status'. (I have a troubled relationship with my parents; I had spots as a teenager; I never had a private education; I lack confidence; I was not popular at school; I couldn't find my dream job, I have an ingrowing toenail, ... etc etc.) And hey presto, I am a self-proclaimed 'outsider'. The fact that I have to proclaim it demonstrates, of course, that I am delusional – an unwittingly conformist, mainstream, brain-washed, delusional. The self-styled free-thinking outsiders of postmodern culture thus constitute a compliant herd of dutiful, submissive sheep dressed as lone wolves. Modern-day Nazareths are full of people hankering for outsider status – who are still repulsed by and still reject anyone who actually *is* a genuine outsider.

There was nothing enviable or glamorous about an outsider in a pre-modern culture. Being expelled from your hometown meant that you had no status, no credentials anywhere else. It turned mere survival into a desperate struggle. Non-conformity today is cool. To our ancestors it was shameful. For us it is cost-free. For them it was life-threatening. And from the outset, Jesus' own life was under precisely this threat.

It is partly for this reason he was deemed 'holy'. In the Bible, holy really means different/set apart/other. It refers to those who refuse to be contaminated by the prevailing ideologies that dehumanise us. Naturally, for an ideology to function properly it must remain largely invisible, undetectable. The modern creed that we live in a 'post-ideological' world is the greatest ideology of all. *We* see the world as it really is. *They* are less enlightened. *We* have learned to tolerate *their* naivety and stupidity. *They* don't need to be heard, only tolerated. This means that *we* are blissfully confined within our impenetrable worldview (whilst retaining the self-congratulatory language of openness/curiosity/tolerance). *They* are people whose views we already know, so we need not interact with them. But *they* are precisely the people to whom Jesus goes, the outsiders, the strangers, the shit of the earth.

The time had come for Jesus to implement his manifesto. To fulfil the words of the prophet Isaiah. To become a means by which the God of heaven takes human form. To do that, he commits himself from the outset to those who are outside/set apart/different. It is to these societal rejects that he comes, and in so doing fulfils the demands of holiness. By shamelessly embracing the other, he has invoked the wrath of his fellow Nazarenes – who have expunged him from their community as they would rid themselves of faecal matter. Hence the righteous profundity of the phrase, 'Holy Shit'. It has always been the hallmark of the true followers of Jesus.

TWELVE LIEUTENANTS

Jesus' campaign was well underway before he withdrew to the mountains to select the twelve. This act was a parody of Israel's traditional leadership model. The title he confers on them ('apostles' or 'envoys') is a highly honoured leadership role – twelve individuals to represent the twelve tribes of Israel. But these men were not leaders from palaces. They were peasants, unpersons huddled on a hillside far from the corridors of power. They had little in the way of privilege, education or influence – but they embodied something of the alternative politics Jesus would offer to his people.

> *Jesus went up on the mountainside and summoned those he wanted, and they came to him. He appointed twelve, so that they might be with him and that he might send them out to campaign and to have authority to drive out demons. These are the twelve he appointed: Simon (to whom he gave the name Peter), James son of Zebedee and his brother John (to them he gave the name Boanerges, which means 'sons of thunder'), Andrew, Philip, Bartholomew, Matthew, Thomas, James son of Alphaeus, Thaddaeus, Simon the Zealot and Judas Iscariot, who handed him over.*
> *(Mark 3:13-19)*

The twelve disciples were unpersons. They never occupied a portacabin, but it is impossible to imagine that they were unfamiliar with portacabin scenarios outlined in previous sections. Many of them were peasant tradesfolk, after all. As with any interpretation of ancient characters, my claims here risk anachronism – but far less so than every subconscious conception of a Jesus who led a fart-less fellowship of followers.

Though my experience is restricted to Western social groups, whether I have been surrounded by military personnel on exercise, riggers on an oil refinery, scaffolders on a coffee break, boy scouts on a camp, or school kids on the playground – farting is universally a common language. Disgust, amusement, admiration and pride are often expressed at the volume and putridity of odours shared, and serve almost as a hierarchy of hands in a game of poker: the climactic build-up to a disappointing feline 'flit'; the anti-climactic moment of an apologetic squeak; the proud trumpet blast that asserts itself instantaneously but whose effects are odourless; the covert but rancid rim-slide that overwhelms its victims one by one; the curious voice from the hindquarters that seems to pose a question; the muffled rhythmic clatter producing a stench that necessitates immediate evacuation of the premises; the machine gun fire with so much ammunition that an inspection is required at once; the moistened squelch that betokens the certainty of liquidic leakage; and finally – the royal flush – anything that evokes the reaction, 'you wanna get that looked at'.

Because of the central role the 'apostles' have played in western literature and art, it is all too easy to picture Jesus' companions as bishops meeting beneath the cloistered vaulting of a palace, senators gathered in the marble corridors of Rome, aristocrats debating in the quiet lounge of a gentleman's club, or politicians negotiating at a G7 summit. But the twelve had no power. Jesus' disciples were neither wealthy nor influential, neither trained in modern social etiquette, nor constrained by the iron-clad laws of English politeness. They were unpersons. And history has not been able to cope well with unpersons gaining a powerful voice.

The annals of Christian history (endorsed by unreflective atheist critiques of that history) have thus transformed the rough-necked tradesmen of Lower Galilee into sophisticated magnates worthy of their place in history. The most effective means of disabusing ourselves of these unconscious, unhistorical distortions is to meet with the twelve in the metaphorical portacabin – an interpretive method overlooked by those biblical interpreters who, as a result of piety or privilege, have never dared to venture into such a seemingly vulgar environment.

The twelve were Palestinian peasant folk, artisans and farmers, on a Mediterranean diet, who would be under no compulsion to clench their buttocks just because Jesus was present. This is the principal social context portrayed by the Gospels – a small group of young men – living and travelling in close mutual proximity. Numbering twelve, they represent the twelve tribes of Israel and thereby the nation as a whole. They were appointed to be *apostles* but a better translation is *lieutenants,* that is, those commissioned to embody the authority of the one who sent them. Why had Jesus selected people like this, and why had they left everything to follow him? Jesus and the twelve were from Lower Galilee, a political backwater surrounding the great lake of the same name. Had Jesus wanted to maximise the impact of his message he would have gone to the cities, found men of good repute, priests, scribes, synagogue leaders, individuals with wealth and influence. This, after all, was the strategy in the Christendom era: firstly, gain influence by all means possible, so that secondly you might use that influence for good. Unfortunately, the process of gaining influence this way changes one's very conception of 'good'. (This is why Jesus had refused to bow before the devil in his second test). The rough neck twelve whom Jesus appointed had no credentials but themselves and their personal stories.

As shown above, Jesus' overall mission was to liberate his people from the degradations of marginalisation and poverty, and his followers were thus the shit of the earth. Despite the prevailing historical myths we have been force-fed, liberating folk from poverty is rarely if ever achieved from a position of privilege and power. It is rather 'from below' that people of privilege and power have been forced to make concessions. Justice (usually translated into the spiritualised, individualised concept, 'righteousness' in English translations of the Bible), is only, ever, always, prized out of the hand of those with power. Jesus surrounded himself with twelve unpersons, because he believed that God could work through unpersons. In fact, the teaching of the Gospel is that, in the person of Jesus, God himself had become an unperson.

Why would the twelve, or anyone else for that matter, follow a nobody like Jesus, the peasant builder from the village of Nazareth?

It is impossible to know, although it probably was not his charm. Most of Jesus' recorded conversations portray him gratuitously and relentlessly criticizing people. Nor would it have been his miracles. He didn't perform any (miracles are a Latin concept alien to whatever Jesus was up to – but more on that later). He probably embodied some kind of rugged charisma – because his followers from Lower Galilee were not gullible, or naïve, and nor would they have been easily impressed. They knew hunger and suffering, and were familiar with the face of death. They had experienced all too deeply the ravages of oppression at the hands of an occupying army. To assume that, because they were peasants from the ancient Mediterranean, they were gullible, ill-informed and unreflective is to project one's own unacknowledged character traits onto historical figures. Most likely they followed this Jesus because he embodied not only charisma, but also some form of authenticity and authority.

They cannot have been easily offended (given how often Jesus lays into them). Nor can Jesus, for that matter, since he seems to be constantly tearing out his hair at their behaviour. Given that kind of relationship, and that kind of people, if they couldn't fart in his presence, he would not be the kind of person they could follow. It is extremely difficult to imagine that he was too proud to fart in their company. Every portrayal of this company is idealised: movies and TV programmes have soundtracks that romanticise them; artistic representations are so heaven-centred their humanity is bracketed out; Christian books have tended to be preoccupied with some spiritual principle that the bodily realities are ignored; even the Bible texts record a highly select portion of words and events. To understand those words and events we must hear them in the gritty, stinking, unpleasant realities of their own context because only then do they have anything to say to ours.

The New Testament is brutally honest about the humanity of the apostles. In the Gospels, they tend to appear only to say stupid things and make stupid mistakes. They are not the charismatic superstar orators we might imagine.

They belonged in the portacabin where they would laugh and argue, joke and complain, belch and fart. Jesus, the builder from Nazareth, was one of them.

WATER INTO WINE

John's Gospel is very different in language and tone to the other three Gospels, Matthew, Mark and Luke. John – probably written deliberately for a non-Palestinian readership – focuses largely on Jesus as a representative of God himself. The so-called miracles or 'signs' as John describes them, are designed to draw attention to something beyond the world of the immediate. They are by no means 'proof' that Jesus was supernatural. Instead, they are an invitation to see, and then to adopt, an alternative view of the world. The incident of turning water into wine took place at an early stage of Jesus' Galilean campaign, and was the first of his great 'signs'.

On the third day there was a wedding in Cana of Galilee, and Jesus was there. Both Jesus and his disciples were invited to the wedding. When the wine ran out, the mother of Jesus said to him, 'They have no wine. And Jesus said to her, 'Woman, what does that have to do with us? My time has not yet come.' His mother said to the servants, 'Do whatever he tells you.'

Now there were six stone water jars set for the Jewish custom of purification, each containing twenty or thirty gallons. Jesus said to them, 'Fill the water jars with water.' So they filled them up to the brim. And he said to them, 'Draw some out now and take it to the head steward.' So they took it to him. When the steward tasted the water which had become wine, and did not know where it came from (but the servants who had drawn the water knew). He called the bridegroom, and said

to him, 'Everyone serves the good wine first, and when the people have drunk freely, then he serves the poorer wine; but you have kept the good wine until now.' This was the first of the signs Jesus did in Cana of Galilee, and manifested His glory, and his disciples believed in him.
(John 2:1-11)

During my first week at Oxford, our pastoral tutor invited all his first-year students to a 'Cheese and Wind' party. In my imagination, this changed completely the meaning of the polite request that we 'RSVP' (roughly translated, 'respond, if it pleases you'). As newcomers, some of us wondered what manner of sophisticated discourse we were destined to exchange at this esteemed university. Maybe the city of dreamy spires and picturesque quadrangles was not so removed from the world of the portacabin where I felt at home. Certainly, the flatulistic display I attended at the end of one wine-filled evening in the bowels of the Oxford College where I studied, trumps every other performance I have witnessed to date.

Students had decamped from the dining hall to an undergraduate room, where they demanded proof that our friend (who went on to become a professional comedian) could – as he claimed – fart on demand. The self-proclaimed flatulist in question was cordially compelled to put his money where his arse is. He obliged. Unceremoniously he took up position on the floor in the centre of the room, folded his legs behind his head and rattled his cack-flaps with over thirty high-volume, high-octane snort-howls, each one with the clarity and magnitude of a rhino-blowing its nose. He ceased his recital only when one of the guests became offended. The flatulist appeared to have astonishing control of his rectal muscles, allowing him to inhale – at will – through his anus, in order that he might then exhale in splendid odourless voice. The performance was fantastic and impressive, even if the farts themselves lacked authenticity and substance (thank God).

Jesus was attending a wedding in a village near to his home (Cana was about an hour's trek from Nazareth), along with his family and his disciples. These events could run over several days, and would have been attended by the whole village, plus folk from beyond. (Presumably, attendance was somewhere in the region of 100-200, though we cannot be sure). At some point, the wine had run out – which seemed particularly distressing to Jesus' middle-aged mother. You can almost hear Jesus roll his eyes as he responds to her anxiety. What follows reveals Jesus' blatant disregard for the laws of social etiquette and chemical fusion. Jesus, so it seems, had conjured up somewhere between 120 and 180 gallons of fine wine, probably around a thousand modern (75cl) bottles. In all likelihood, this amounts to several bottles per person. Bearing in mind that wedding guests had already been supplied with wine and would thus have been generously lubricated, the effects of several extra bottles per head may well have been toxic.

What is more – up until this point in the feast, guests had been knocking back Lambrusco from Morrisons. The wedding steward is thus astonished to learn that – now the guests are already intoxicated – the groom had been sitting on a reserve wine cellar comprised of Château Lafitte. If the best wine has been saved until last, the guests will want to keep drinking. And it is worth dwelling briefly on the effects. A crowd of guests have ingested copious amounts of fine wine. There is an irony that the jars from which they were poured usually contained water for the process of attaining personal purity. Once that wine is ingested, the effects might be deemed anything other than purifying. The wine had travelled through the oesophagus and into the stomach, from where some of the alcohol is absorbed straight into the blood stream. The rest of the alcohol travels to the small intestine, and makes its way into the liver – which prepares to jettison the alcohol molecules from the body. Eventually, once these 'grapes of wrath' had completed their journey through the bodies of wedding guests, their exit strategies would include sweat, headache, hangover, urine, faeces, and of course – flatulence.

The bible describes this curious event as a 'sign' – so what is its significance? We do best to consider this from the practice adopted by the early church. Long before 'Holy Communion' or 'Eucharist' was reduced to the practice of a sip of wine and a bread crumb (unwitting symbols of God's lack of generosity), Christians would come together to share a proper meal. That meal included bread and wine. Every member of the community brought something. If you were an orphan, you brought water because you could afford nothing else. If you were wealthy, you brought your best bottle of Château Lafitte. Most were somewhere in the middle. All the liquid was poured into a single vat, and then redistributed as a cup of wine to every individual. The distinction between haves and have-nots was obliterated. The meal was a demonstration of radical solidarity. When everyone recited the liturgical claim, 'though we are many, we are one,' they were telling the truth. The poorest members of the community contributed water, and they drank wine.

That is radical solidarity. The poorest members of society were not socially distanced from the wealthiest. By contrast, for most modern westerners, suffering is carefully packaged long before it arrives in our consciousness. When it appears on our screen, it is already framed as something 'out there', distant from us, calling us to feel some sentiment – perhaps enough to move us as far as flicking small amounts of cash into a digitalised charity collection plate. But this is the moral equivalent of dealing with suffering by attempting to inhale it anally. We need not be genuinely confronted by the plight of others so as to have an impact on who we are in relation to them. We need not, in other words, digest – and process through our entire being – the tragic plight of others. This is the Selfie-stick solidarity of the modern era, is a performance that is fantastic and impressive, but a performance that lacks authenticity and substance.

For our ancestors in the early Christian communities, *they* were not the objects of *our* charity, *our* altruism, *our* generosity – because *they* were *us*. Our wellbeing was rooted in theirs. We shared a common cup. This is a long, long way from the selfie-stick solidarity: where I speak on behalf of poor people without ever taking the trouble to listen to them; where poor people exist to provide me with a photo-opportunity; where poverty tourism makes me feel better whilst having a negative real-world impact; where people can admire my benevolence, but where my self-indulgent use of vulnerable folk remains unchallenged; where poor folk boost my ego, without disturbing my lifestyle; where I get all the sentimental benefits with none of the emotional cost. Selfie-stick solidarity can thus feel genuine and arise from well-meaning motives – but it is a way of engaging with poverty that keeps poor people at a safe distance from who we really are. It is to enjoy wine (throughout Israel's history, a symbol of economic wellbeing) and turn it into water. It is to drink from the well of Western privilege, then piss all over the poor and call it virtue.

THE LEPER'S DARE

Social distancing was a moral necessity in Jesus' day. To keep society free of contamination from contact with sinners, you simply had to avoid physical contact. Jesus had a reckless disregard for this convention. Time and again in the Gospels, we hear that when he is confronted with a person or a situation, their plight reaches straight into his bowels where a hurricane begins to turn. The biblical word for this experience is 'compassion'. Once that storm has commenced, Jesus steam-rolls through any cultural convention to engage in full-blown compassionate physicality with the person in front of him. A leper, however, is the last person in God's holy land that any holy man would touch.

> *A man with leprosy came to Jesus and begged him on his knees, 'If you dared to, you could make me clean.'*
>
> *Jesus felt his own bowels twist. He reached out his hand and touched the man. 'I dare', he said. 'Be clean! Immediately the leprosy left him and he was cleansed.*
>
> *Jesus sent him away at once with a strong warning: 'Make sure that you don't tell this to anyone. Instead, go and show yourself to the priest and offer the sacrifices that Moses commanded for your cleansing, as a testimony to them.'*
>
> *Instead, he went out and began to talk freely, spreading the news. As a result, Jesus could no longer enter a town openly but stayed outside in lonely places. And still, the people still came to him from everywhere.*
>
> *(Mark 1:40-45)*

The 'Senior Combination Room' (SCR) of an Oxford college is where academics relax, exchange intellectual chit-chat, drink coffee and read broadsheet newspapers. The rooms are magnificent, providing a civilized environment and inviting strict if unwritten behavioural etiquette. One Sunday afternoon in the early 2000s I happened to venture into the beautiful Georgian SCR of a college (that will remain anonymous) to obtain a nice coffee from the machine. Since it was a weekend, the SCR was empty, leaving me free of the usual behavioural constraints. After a busy morning in Chapel, I grabbed a copy of the *Guardian*, sank into a leather armchair, and released my intestinal gasses into the intellectual atmosphere. The result was lengthy, thunderous and satisfying: a proud sabbatical ass-clatter which sounded like its very own hearty round of applause. All was well in the world. Until to my horror – from one of the alcoves – I heard the rustling of a newspaper page turning.

Discovering I was not alone, I glanced over and hidden behind the *Daily Telegraph* sat a very eminent professor of criminology (whom I had never officially met). He seemed unperturbed by my crime. Had he heard me? Of course he had – but his silence was excruciating. I sank behind my *Guardian* – an excellent tool for concealing capital offences. After a minute or so, I decided to sneak out but at that very moment, as if in reply, from behind the *Telegraph* came a confident and worthy posterial tremor of symphonic proportion – worthy of a standing ovation.

Only silence followed.

After another minute or so the *Telegraph* rustled with another page turn and I withdrew with a due sense of shame, gratitude and admiration. It was the only conversation I ever exchanged with the professor, but I always held him in very high regard. Having read the situation clearly, he was sufficiently attuned to my embarrassment to allow his empathy to transgress social convention.

Jesus did not perform 'drive-by' healings. He did not heal everyone he met and – contrary to *The Life of Brian*, he did not heal random people 'without so much as a "by your leave."' Rather, he healed those who came to him – and in this case a man with leprosy approached him. The leper, however, did not ask to be healed. He did not even ask to be made clean. Rather, he dared Jesus to declare him clean. Jesus' response cannot be understood without a little context.

Whether the man suffered leprosy as we understand it today is unknown but unlikely. Rabbis listed 72 different types of skin complaint – including burns, boils, ringworm and scalp conditions. We can be sure, at least, that this leper suffered something a little more serious than heavy dandruff. The various conditions termed as leprosy were viewed as a curse by God and contagious – which meant that those afflicted with the condition were expelled from their communities, reduced to the status of outcast. A cursory glance at the Mosaic regulations imposed on 'lepers' reveals the spiritual, social and physical humiliation to which this man was subject. As a victim of this disease, he was expected to isolate himself from human company, maintain a scruffy and unkempt appearance, and warn others of his approach by shouting out, 'Unclean! Unclean!' (Lev 13:45-46). It is striking then, that this man should walk straight into the town and confront Jesus.

The man, however, longed to be restored to his community. This concern seemed paramount – he wanted Jesus to declare him clean, even though he knew that this might undermine the priests (the only ones certified to issue a clean bill of health). This, in turn, would get Jesus into all kinds of trouble. It was troublesome because if the leper were declared 'clean' he could return to human society, re-attain his dignity, and enjoy being part of his community. But as a leper, such a welcome would be impossible. The 'clean bill of health' obviously presupposed there was no longer any trace of leprosy. The man with leprosy had issued a dangerous challenge to Jesus. He had dared Jesus to declare him clean. Confronted with this desperate man, who recognised in Jesus a self-authenticating authority, Jesus reveals his vulnerability. He felt his response in his intestines – his bowels loosened. Such was the strength of his unease with the situation.

Before examining this reaction further, it is worth re-emphasizing that in Hebrew thought, the bowel (rather than the heart) was the seat of human emotion. So that when Israel's great prophets speak about an experience that moves the bowels of God (e.g., Isa 16:11; 63:15; Jer 31:20; cf 2 Cor 7:15;

Phil 1:8 etc), it is not to be taken literally. Nevertheless, it pays to reflect on the sheer 'earthiness' of ancient Hebrew thought. The colourful, graphic, realist imagery of Hebrew language (a churning in the bowels) makes our own modern alternatives (a fluttering heart, butterflies in the tummy) seem shallow and inadequate by comparison.

The modern age is irrationally obsessed with rationality. As such it struggles to account for the enormity of the role that the non-rational has in shaping our human identity. Often, especially when it comes to ethics, we are then compelled to 'rationalise' the decisions, the assumptions and the mistakes we have made because we made them for emotional reasons. In modern thought, we are trained to keep (or at least, to think we can keep) emotions away from the driving seat of our lives and cultures (which prevents us from acknowledging the role they actually play).

By contrast, Hebrew ethics accepted a central role for our emotions, to embrace them and – where possible – to address them, to train them, to channel them. The language of feeling our bowels move in reaction to situations that confront us, feels entirely wholesome. It recognises that our full-bodied, red-blooded personhood – in all its embarrassing complexity – is fully engaged when we act humanely.

It may help to appreciate the difference by reflecting on popular modern phrases that address 'the heart'. In each case, it will be instructive to replace the word 'heart' with 'bowels': So, for instance, if you love someone with 'all your bowels', then you really do mean it. To 'eat your bowls out' would be a meal without a happy ending; a 'bowel-to-bowl' conversation belongs well and truly in the portacabin (though I had just enjoyed one with an eminent professor); and should you wish to 'open your bowels' in order to 'pour your bowels out', then things are going to get messy.

Modern rationality has become so compartmentalised that it is difficult to feel our way into a story like this, and to appreciate fully the basic mortal experiences of the human Jesus. Bowel movements, churning guts, can be a direct consequence of an emotionally healthy approach to engaging with other people. Jesus was no dispassionate divinity, drifting around ancient Palestine on a do-gooding mission in which he blanket-bombed the world with miraculous healing, simply because he could. Jesus was not dispassionate – he was a bloke, moved in his guts and courageous enough to allow his empathy to transgress social convention.

At the very outset of his messianic enterprise, Jesus' bowels are very much in the driving seat of his campaign.

THE DEMON-POSSESSED CHILD

Whilst in Galilee, Jesus seems to have spent a lot of time casting out demons. All we may surmise from the Gospel, is that an individual's psyche had been conquered by an alien host. Victims were thus utterly dehumanised. It is interesting that once Jesus quits Galilee, he encounters hardly any demons. It may well be, then, that demon possession was a personal manifestation of the oppression inflicted on an entire region at the hands of brutal overlords. When Jesus encounters this, he employs none of the recognised strategies used by other exorcists. Instead, he simply radiates a presence that these hostile spirits cannot withstand.

When they returned to the disciples, they saw a large crowd around them, and some scribes arguing with them. Immediately, when the whole crowd saw Jesus, they were astonished and began running to greet Him. And he asked them, 'What are you discussing with them?' Someone in the crowd answered, 'Teacher, I brought you my son, possessed by a spirit that makes him unable to speak. Whenever it seizes him, it slams him to the ground and he foams at the mouth, grinds his teeth, and turns rigid. I told your disciples to exorcise it, but they could not.'

He answered them, saying, 'You disloyal generation, how long must I be with you? How long must I tolerate you? Bring him to me!' They brought the boy to him. When he saw him, immediately the spirit threw him into a convulsion and – falling to the ground – he started rolling around and foaming from the mouth.

Jesus asked the father, 'How long has this been going on?' And he said,

'From childhood. It has often thrown him both into the fire and into the water to kill him. So if you can do anything, move your bowels and help us!' Jesus replied, '"If you can?" All things are possible to one who is loyal.'

Immediately the boy's father shouted, 'I am loyal! Help me overcome any disloyalty.'

When Jesus saw that the crowd was swelling, he rebuked the unclean spirit, 'You deaf and mute spirit, I command you, come out of him and never re-enter him.'

After shouting and throwing him into horrible convulsions, it came out; and the boy became so much like a corpse that most of them said, 'He's dead!'

But Jesus took him by the hand, lifted him, and he got up. When he came into the house, his disciples started quizzing him privately, 'Why couldn't we drive it out?' He told them, 'This kind cannot come out by anything but prayer.'

(Mark 9:14-29)

A generation ago, an article in the British Medical Journal noted that, 'from infancy the British are brought up to regard a daily bowel action as almost a religious necessity' (BMJ 1980, 669). Various studies have since emphasized a British preoccupation with and pride at regularizing the movements of their own bowels. As we have seen, from a first century Jewish perspective, this regimented bowel-control would be closely related to emotional control. In this light, the British reputation for maintaining a 'stiff upper lip' is inseparable from the religious discipline that regulates the south-facing lower lips of the *Asinus Britannica*. But being 'anally retentive' (in the non-Freudian interpersonal sphincter-clenching sense) is by no means exclusive to modern day British folk. In fact, the phrase, 'stiff upper lip' has its origins not in Britain at all, but in the 19th Century US. Similarly, modern US citizens have inherited a cultural embarrassment in describing even the private location for bowel movements – namely as 'the restroom' – presumably because of a stiffened lower-lip. I suspect few Americans go to such a place for a quick nap. I have yet to hear an American describe the human-waste-disposal-chamber of their house in the functional terms my British portacabin colleagues employ: the crapper, the bog, the trap, the shit house etc.

The story of the demon-possessed boy is a story about control of bowel movements. Whatever first century Mediterranean peasants regarded as demon-possession is far beyond the radar of modern attempts to categorise the phenomenon as reported in the Gospels. It is highly likely however, that – here and there – a certain individual unperson in a land subjected to imperial oppression might become a tragic, personal embodiment of the hostile takeover to which their land and people had been subjected. Their lives become a hopeless public display of the fate of their people.

The boy in the story above appears to fulfil this purpose. He is silenced, overcome, downcast, convulsive, frustrated, immobilized, and – later in the story – lifeless. Is this not the fate of any nation occupied by tyrants who abuse, mistreat, and drain its resources and its people? It is probably for this reason that when his disciples are unable to rid the boy of this alien spirit, Jesus rebukes not them, but the entire generation. It seems like an unwarranted accusation, unless this boy's condition is a symptom of his entire generation. This is no harsh rebuke of the disciples' shortcoming, but of a nation that cannot respond better when being subject to occupation. The implicit claim is that the nation the boy represents, need not be subjected to any of the symptoms he manifests. Despite being overcome by a pagan superpower, Israel is not thereby rendered voiceless and vanquished, ground down and subject to convulsive despair, paralysis, and death. These responses are felt only by those who believe that the only form of liberation available is to overthrow their oppressors by force of arms – a pointless and impossible hope.

According to Jesus' logic, faithful Israel should know better. The liberation he offers is not salvation from hardship but is made real even in the very midst of such brutal oppression. His prophecies will detail alternative means of overthrowing oppression without resorting to futile militarism. But for now, Jesus is confronted with an urgent personal situation. The boy's father has challenged him to show mercy/have compassion. Once again, the imagery used is that of the bowels moving, the guts twisting and Jesus feeling in every fibre of his being, the tragedy of the boy's plight. Jesus confronts and expels the evil spirit, but not before this poor boy has been brought apparently to the point of death. The language of the boy's restoration is that of resurrection and spells broader hope not so much that Jesus can perform healing for many individuals, but that he might effect an entire nationwide form of liberation.

The key element of the story, however, is the insight that this kind of demon can be exorcised only by 'prayer'. This needs to be properly understood. It's not as though the disciples of Jesus did not pray. Nor that the nation of Israel did not pray. Standard procedure for exorcism did not usually include prayer, however – but this does not mean that some bible thumping religious fruitcake of an exorcist has to ask God for a bit of help, as though they were having trouble pushing out a mighty brätwurst of a turd. The word used for prayer is rooted in the practice of making a vow (a 'euche' in Greek). When that vow is actively and carefully directed towards ('pro-') a great Other, it becomes 'proseuche' – prayer. The underlying notion is quite close to Scarlet O'Hara's famous line, 'As God is my witness, they're not going to lick me'. The imagery is of a radical commitment you have made from the bowels, engaging every fibre of your being, and implicating every atom of the cosmos. This, after all, is the extent to which Jesus himself felt the plight of the poor boy at the centre of this incident.

Regulating one's bowels, however, prevents one's entire being from engaging fully in the human responsibilities that present themselves to the people of God. It is for this reason that the author of John's letters later in the New Testament asks how a Christian with resources at his disposal can then see fellow humans in need and 'shutteth his bowels' towards him (I John 3:17). The metaphor relates to the compassion one might feel towards another. But here it may be helpful to distinguish a sentimental from an emotional reaction. An emotional reaction to the suffering of others manifests itself in action because it penetrates every fibre of your being. A sentimental reaction however (at least, what I mean by sentimental) enables those who indulge in it to experience all the positive and gooey feelings, with none of the actual cost. A sentimental reaction can tug at my heartstrings. I may even reach for the tissues, as when I see *Toy Story III* or listen to the *Pearl Harbour* soundtrack. But sentimentalism does not drive me to any kind of world-changing action, even if it leaves me with the self-assuredness that I care. No matter how many tissues the momentum of my weeping takes me through, my upper lip remains stiff and my bowels remain closed. In John's view, a daily bowel action might – after all – truly be a religious necessity.

THE HEALING OF A LEGION

Jesus goes out onto the great Lake of Galilee (around 13 miles long and 8 miles wide). After having calmed a storm on the Lake (silencing it like he silences demons), he lands on the Eastern shore, pagan territory. Soon after disembarking, he is confronted by a man who appears to have had his life wrecked by an entire brigade of demons that have taken control of him.

> *Then they arrived at the country of the Gerasenes, which is opposite Galilee. When Jesus stepped on land, a man from the city greeted him, [a man] who had demons. For some time he had worn no clothes, and he lived not in a house but among the tombs. When he saw Jesus, he shouted out and fell down before him, and said with a loud voice, 'What do you have to do with me, Jesus, Son of the Most High God? I beg you, do not torment me.' For Jesus had commanded the unclean spirit to come out of the man. (It had often seized him. He was kept under guard and restrained with chains and fetters, but he would break the restraints and be driven by the demon into the desert). Jesus then demanded of him, 'What is your name?' And he said 'Legion' because many demons had entered him. And they were begging Jesus not to send them into the abyss. Now a large herd of pigs was feeding there on the hillside; and they begged Jesus to let them enter these. So he allowed them. Then the demons came out of the man and entered the swine, and the herd charged down the steep bank into the lake and were drowned. When the herdsmen saw what had happened, they fled, and*

reported it throughout the city and in the country. When people went out to see what had happened, they came to Jesus and found the man from whom the demons had gone, sitting at the feet of Jesus, clothed and sober-minded – and they were afraid. And those who had seen it told them how the man who had been possessed with demons was healed. Then all the people of the surrounding country of the Gerasenes asked him to leave; for they were seized by great fear; so he got into the boat and returned. The man from whom the demons had gone begged that he might stay with him; but he released him, saying, 'Return to your household and tell the story of how much God has done for you.' And he went away, proclaiming throughout the whole city how much Jesus had done for him.

(Luke 8:26-39)

Anyone who has attended a church regularly for any number of years will have stories of how moments of collective, reflective silence have been interrupted by the seismic rectal tremors of guilty worshippers. The severity is often accentuated by the architectural structure of a church building. Take pews. These are the wooden benches, seating up to a dozen folk on one piece of material. In the event of a Christian arse-quake, this lengthy plank of varnished hardwood can serve as an acoustic amplifier, broadcasting your private shame throughout the congregation. Since everyone is sat in a row, often with some kind of enclosure at either end, it is impossible to identify the culprit. The judders, however, may reverberate along the entire length of the pew. For those who are unfortunately well-positioned the vibrations from your fellow worshipper's buttocks can be felt directly through your own. It is a unique bond of fellowship.

In the few seconds of grace that follow, you may quickly pray that an odourless wonder has occurred and hope to God that the stench of demonic cabbage, satanic egg or diabolically wadded beef does not make a liturgical intrusion via the pipe of your brother's rectal organ.

I recall an incident in a Norfolk Chapel, where at the end of the prayer of confession the minister invited the congregation to pause in silence in order to feel the forgiveness God had granted. It was a genuinely powerful moment of quietude, until the howl of the ass-claxon sounded. Never before had I heard such clear-cut enunciation from a human's lower mouthpiece. The ecclesiastical eruption manifested itself as a rear-end squawk akin to an air-raid siren: it began slow and burbling, gradually rising in tempo, volume and pitch before eventually whining back down into a deep rumble that may well have registered on the Richter scale. While most worshippers dutifully struggled to suppress their amusement, some believed they had been witnesses to an anal exorcism. If evil spirits had voices, surely this is how they would scream when ejected from the body of their victim.

It is highly like the story of the demon possessed man from our Gospel reading was one such story. The symptoms listed bear a striking resemblance to what is currently called post-traumatic stress – and the treatment given him, runs in striking correspondence to the those offered today to victims of combat trauma. The language is thoroughly militaristic: The name 'Legion' refers only to a military unit; the collective description for the swineherd was not usually used of pigs, but of bands of military recruits; the charge into the lake is the word used for a battle charge. And the region was occupied by the Tenth Legion, who bore on their standard, the head of a pig. This was a region brutalised time and again by the Romans in the first century.

If Legion is indeed a personal embodiment of the military abuses inflicted upon a people, then we may assume he had suffered first-hand his own personal experience of violent trauma. If cosmological demonic forces have imposed injustice, humiliation and trauma on the populace, then those forces have all come raging through the shattered psyche of this solitary human life. The American Psychiatric association lists four symptom groups – all of which are consistent with the suffering of Legion. This struck me as I once read accounts of victims of combat trauma from the Vietnam war – so I will quote some of those accounts which add flesh to the symptoms suffered by Legion.

Firstly, this man was not born demon possessed – but had only suffered this trauma for a defined period of time. After his healing he was free to return to his household. Something had happened to him. As one former soldier has declared: 'Why I became like that? It was all evil. All evil. Where before, I wasn't. I look back, I look back today and I'm horrified at what I turned into. What I was. What I did. I just look at it like it was somebody else... It was somebody else. Somebody had control of me' (Shay, *Achilles in Vietnam*, 1995, 33).

That the man lived among the tombs, may speak of survivor guilt felt by so many. Obsession with the dead can feel as though it makes former comrades present. As another Vietnam survivor said, 'I never expected to return home alive, and emotionally never have' (Shay, 1995, 73).

The rage felt by Legion, was plain to see. Neither guards nor chains were sufficient to restrain the demonic power that surged through him, driving him away from human society and into the desert. Again, these three aspects of the man's behaviour are echoed frequently by today's victims of PTSD, as exemplified by the war veteran who often underwent (a) the un-metaphorical experience of being seized by a 'monster,' (b), with violent results and (c), consequent isolation: 'Every three days I would totally explode, lose it for no reason at all. I'd be sitting there calm as could be, and this monster would come out of me with a fury most people didn't want to be around. So it wasn't just over there [in Vietnam]. I brought it back here with me' (Shay, 1995, 33).

The fall-out from this incident could not have been instantaneous. The herdsmen had to flee, spread word in the city and in the surrounding country – actions that would at least take several hours. Presumably, the healer spent some of those hours establishing what the therapist Judith Herman describes the first of three stages of recovery from trauma: an environment of safety, sober-mindedness and self-care. By the time the crowds arrived on the scene, that first stage appeared to be well underway, since they witnessed for themselves the man from whom the demons had gone no longer prostrate but sitting at the feet of Jesus, no longer naked but clothed, no longer tormented but sober-minded.

The second instruction from Jesus is to tell the story of what God has done for him. Not to preach, not to report the incident which was already widely known. But to tell the story. This is the second stage of trauma recovery.

Since such trauma victims usually have a dislocated sense of time – with a debilitating sense of past, a total lack of future, and an inability to escape the present – the discipline of telling the true story of who he was would be a profoundly difficult challenge for this man. The injunction to 'tell the story' may thus be understood as one of ongoing therapy, because the story of this man's life becomes no longer a fragmented tale of tragedy and trauma, but the story of how much God had done for him.

The third instruction from Jesus is to send him home. The man begged to go with Jesus, but Jesus instructed him to return to his household. This instruction prefigures the third element of recovery noted by Herman, namely 'reconnection', i.e., being reintegrated as part of his community, an environment in which the man is supported, heard, affirmed and above all, known. Such an environment would be a necessary part of the story of his healing: 'the poorly understood "spontaneous", or "natural," processes of recovery that happen in the native soil of a veteran's own community' (Shay, *Odysseus in America*, 2003, 5). The real healing of this man was not simply the dramatic moment of exorcism – but the process Jesus set up, thoroughly in accordance with modern therapeutic models.

FEEDING AN ARMY

Jesus had only recently heard of the death of his cousin, John the Baptist and – according to Mark's Gospel – has not had time to process this tragic news. At this stage, John's influence amongst the Jewish people eclipsed that of Jesus. John was a charismatic leader with a clear message and an enormous following, who had secured his own place in history quite apart from the Gospel narratives. On learning of John's death Jesus goes in search of solitude – probably to grieve the loss of his kinsman and to reflect on the gaping hole this had left in the morale of his people.

The lieutenants gathered around Jesus and reported to him all they had done and taught. Then, because so many people were coming and going that they did not even have a chance to eat, he said to them, 'Come with me by yourselves to a quiet place and get some rest.' So they went away by themselves in a boat to a secluded spot.

But many who saw them leaving recognized them and ran on foot from all the towns and got there ahead of them.

When he landed and saw a large crowd, he was moved in his bowels because of them: they were like sheep without a shepherd.

So he began teaching them many things.

As it got late, his disciples came to him. 'This is a remote place,' they said, 'and it's already getting late. Send the people away so that they can go to the surrounding farms and villages and buy themselves something to eat.'

But he answered, 'Give them something to eat yourselves.'

They said to him, 'That would take more than half a year's wages· Are we to go and spend that much on bread and give it to them to eat?'

'How many loaves do you have?' he asked. 'Go and see.'

When they found out, they told him, 'Five—and two fish.'

Then Jesus instructed them to have all the people sit down in groups on the green grass. So they sat down in groups of hundreds and fifties. Taking the five loaves and the two fish and looking up to heaven, he gave thanks and broke the loaves. Then he gave them to his disciples to distribute to the people. He also divided the two fish among them all. They all ate and were satisfied, and the disciples picked up twelve basketfuls of broken pieces of bread and fish. The number of the men who had eaten was five thousand.

(Mark 6:30-44)

The secular eyes of a voting populace may today witness for themselves how a god can become mortal. That is, how an animated human carcass may become the host of demonic forces hell-bent on extracting unnecessary wealth from a beleaguered population and a planet cooking on gas-mark 9. This is the neoliberal doctrine of the incarnation, where a gigantic immortal corporate identity can acquire a friendly, popular, charming, trustworthy human face-hole to execute its will. The word for this acquisition process is 'leadership'.

A popular political leader in the early 21st century will stand for nothing other than opposing those who dare to stand for something, anything. This toxic conviction-vacuity is in strict accord with the will of wealthy sponsors, powerful lobbyists, and expertly manufactured public opinion. A leader who, in a world entering an advanced state of eco-dystrophy, can motivate the masses to remain disinterested and docile. A leader whose vision is to ensure that the electorate remain visionless. A leader who inspires voters to roll their eyes at anyone who unmasks the true state of the world. A walking corpse plastered with thick make-up and toxic perfume, controlled by the hand of a corporate ventriloquist to whisper sweet nothings at a complacent populace so that even liberal intellectuals join the cheers as the planet burns around them. Leadership.

Then came Trump. But in more than one western democracy, recent history has witnessed what happens when a septic tank acquires millions of dollars, grows limbs, climbs out of the ground, paints a face around its outlet valve and sloshes its way into high office. And yet, despite all their influence, the leader's pitiable desire for the adoration of the crowds remains.

Jesus was seeking seclusion from the crowds but had failed. The multitude was following him in desperation, and when Jesus saw them his bowels turned to a watery whirlpool. The reason being that he saw his own people as '*sheep without a shepherd*'. This kind of reaction might well seem patronising to the modern reader, as Jesus views those poor lost souls who are simply desperate for a messiah such as myself to give them some kind of meaning or purpose. Is he not, after all, viewing these people as 'sheep'? Were we reading about anyone else, we might have little hesitation in diagnosing them with a 'Messiah Complex'. The full metaphor, however, is 'sheep without a shepherd'. This is hardly surprising, given the all-too-recent loss of such a towering figure as John the Baptist. John had been a prophetic titan in his day, arisen from among the people rather than the elites, calling Israel to undergo a radical and revolutionary change of mindset. If Herod Antipas (Galilee's ruler) wanted to maintain the order necessary to keep the taxes rolling in and the Roman overlords content, John had to go. After months of imprisonment at Herod's mountain fortress, he was eventually executed.

It is worth pausing here a moment to listen out for Jesus' bowels. When he sees his own people, beleaguered and bereaved, hopes dashed and stomachs empty – is it any wonder his lower guts turn into a cement-mixer? The experience clearly compelled him to do something, but what? To pronounce himself shepherd to lead his people as though they were herd animals or livestock?

Not. At. All.

Jesus was no opportunist, seizing the moment to declare himself a great leader and step into the limelight. Far from it. He had appointed twelve lieutenants to represent the twelve tribes of Israel – and so instructed *them* to give the people what they need. Whatever the nature of what happened next,

Jesus did not wave a magic wand and produce miraculous food. Instead, he challenges his lieutenants: 'Give them something to eat, YOURSELVES!' The Gospel gives little detail, but the outcome is that from within the people themselves, God himself can provide. All Jesus did was to thank God for what people already had. The symbolism is clear. The economic survival of Israel's people is by no means dependent on puppet kings, imperial overlords, or messianic heroes. These people are not sheep.

Many political thinkers throughout history have marvelled at how the masses of easily governable unpersons (or perhaps, 'sheep') can remain docile in face of their oppressors – especially when they overwhelmingly outnumber their oppressors. Take Livy, a contemporary of Jesus, who narrated the outrageous behaviour of the historic war hero and saviour of Rome, Marcus Manlius (?-384BCE). Having drawn attention to the criminal injustices of his fellow elites, Marcus roused the peasant populace to rebellion, with the words, 'How long must you remain ignorant of your own power?' (*Quo usque tandem ignorabitis vires vestras*). The metaphoric dimension of the parable puts that same question to the Galileans of Jesus' day. He draws them to realise that Israel's God has always located himself in the midst of Israel's people and as such has himself provided what any leader would be expected to provide above all else: bread.

In agrarian societies, those producing bread were treated with special privileges. In England, for instance, the Anglo Saxon 'lord' was originally, the 'loaf ward' – the one responsible for providing bread for people. In the present situation, on the hillside near the Galilean village of Bethsaida, it appears that somehow Israel's God has quietly provided bread for Israel's people. The number of leftover baskets represents the abundance that may be encountered by Israel's twelve tribes when they remain loyal to their God. Jesus made no great public drama and demanded no fanfare so the people could marvel at his leaderly magnificence. Quite the opposite.

This did not prevent the people from attempting to seize him and make him king (John 6:15), leaving Jesus and his bowels having to retreat to the mountains. There were, after all, five thousand men (in addition to women and children), equal in number to the Roman legion stationed in Judea –

and without the need for provisions. To many, this was a sizeable force. But Jesus was not their leader and was by no means presenting himself as their shepherd.

'Strong people,' said civil rights activist, Ella Baker, 'do not need strong leaders.' Of course, they need organization and order, unified goals and passionate commitment. Baker herself was a brilliant grass-roots organizer, and Jesus had issued instructions on how to organise the five thousand (Luke 9:14). But leadership? The devil had already tested Jesus for his kingly leadership credentials, and Jesus had failed royally. As stated above, most would-be leaders would not fail. Those who clamber above all else for influence and power, must gradually surrender their spirit to the interests of those who already wield power. Whether I am driven to become an imperial pretender, an electoral candidate, a journalistic success, an economic entrepreneur, a one-minute manager, an internet influencer, or a church-leader – my success depends on me pouring my heart into my ambition. And once my heart is empty, what will refill it? The sluice-gates of power are ever open, the sewage of its ambition poised to flood in. And hey presto. To become a septic tank full of demonic rectum-slurry is the unwitting ambition of many a well-intentioned would-be leader. And as Jesus had said, 'when the heart is full, the mouth overflows' (Luke 6:45).

THE GOOD SAMARITAN

Lawyers would often confront Jesus with testing questions, not because they were nasty people who wanted to catch him out, but because this was standard Jewish practice. Jesus was a rabbi and, in order to learn, Jewish legal experts would engage in serious, heart-felt debate with him. They would often argue like mad, and then go and share a beer. The lawyer who approached Jesus in this instance was probably well-intentioned, but his question backfires spectacularly to reveal both his expertise and his ignorance.

And look, a lawyer stood up to put him to the test, saying, 'Teacher, what kind of thing should I do to inherit eternal life?' He said to him, 'What is written in the law? How do you interpret?' And he answered, 'You shall love the Lord your God with all your heart, and with all your life, and with all your strength, and with all your mind; and your neighbour as yourself.' So he said to him, 'You have answered correctly. Put this into practice, and you will live.'

But he, wanting to justify himself, said to Jesus, 'So who is my neighbour?'

Jesus replied, 'A certain man was going down from Jerusalem to Jericho, and he fell among robbers, who stripped him down, beat him up, and left him half dead. By chance a priest was going down that road, and when he saw him, he passed by on the other side. In the same way a Levite, when he came to the place and saw him, passed by on the other side. But a Samaritan, as he travelled, came to where he was; and when he saw him, he had compassion, and went to him and bandaged his wounds, pouring on oil and wine; then he set him on his own beast and brought him to a hostel, and took care of him. And the next day he took out two denarii and gave them to the hostel keeper, saying "Look after him, and whatever more you spend I will repay you when I come back." Which of these three do you think proved themselves a neighbour to the man who fell among the robbers?'

He said, 'The one who practiced compassion toward him.'

And Jesus said to him, 'Now you go and put that same thing into practice.'

(Luke 10:25-37)

Stuart and Karen visited a supermarket in Kidlington, soon after late-night opening hours began. An evening visit was their preferred shopping routine, given how quiet the aisles were and how quickly they could run the gauntlet. One evening, towards the end of their shopping, Stuart went ahead to obtain his favourite snack. Whilst facing the biscuits in search of the custard creams (and knowing he and his wife were alone in the aisle) through the corner of his eye he waited for her to draw near. With impeccable timing, he proudly discharged an omnipotent cheek-burning fire-cracker followed momentarily by malodorous after-shock. Without turning, he grimaced audibly. Then, with his free hand, wafted the methanic vapours from his backside in the direction of Karen, and proudly chuckled, 'put that in your pipe and smoke it.' He turned to watch her reaction, only to learn that the woman walking behind him was not Karen at all – but a startled looking woman he recognised from a few aisles earlier. Contents from his anal cavity entered the nasal cavity of the innocent passer-by. It *presupposed a mutual familiarity they did not share,* which is why farting is often just plain wrong.

This link between one person's bowels and another's lungs is a profoundly human tie, which hangs a question mark over the social delicacies of modern civilization. Modern civilized society (see Introduction) is based on how firstly an independent free-thinking 'I' then decides to relate to separate, isolated 'other' somewhere out there beyond me. In Hebrew thought – which takes place not only in the rational mind but in one's entire body – the 'other' need not be so distant.

The Lawyer who approached Jesus wanted to identify which neighbour, what kind of 'other' was a worthy object of his love. (By love here, is meant that state when my wellbeing depends entirely on that of someone else). The question evokes one of Jesus' best-known parables, in which he does not answer the lawyer's question (who is *my* neighbour?) but questions the lawyer's answer (to whom have *you proven yourself* a neighbour?). Samaritans were hated outsiders, drawing out from the best and brightest in Israel whatever xenophobic instincts might be lingering in their psyche. It is easy for modern egalitarian liberals to distance themselves from such xenophobic tendencies. When reading a story of Samaritan heroism, of defying expectations and crossing social boundaries, it is easy for modern readers to identify themselves with the hero. Of course, I would not be like one of those dastardly racist religious types (Priests and Levites). Of course, I would act like the Good Samaritan. Of course, I would help anyone in need. Jesus uses the Samaritan's bowels as the driving force of his response.

As Brian Brock has it,

> The parable of the Good Samaritan pivots on the line, 'when he saw him, he was moved in his bowels.' The story ends by summarizing the response to this inner movement as a 'showing of mercy.' The Hebraism translated into Greek used here, splanchnizesthai—'to be deeply moved' as in 'deeply in the bowels,' appears at several crucial points in the gospels. Jesus is depicted as a being living inside the tent of his skin in a manner that ensures that his outer surfaces are sensitive to the truth of an embodied person. A depth of bodily connection between human beings is powerfully evoked. Jesus calls everyone to receive this heightened sensitivity. (Brock and Byassee, *Disability*, 2021)

Brock draws attention to 'the aggregate of impressions arising from organic sensations.' It highlights the sheer importance of the gritty, full-blown bodilyness of our knowledge, our thinking, our theories and our actions. This is largely at odds with modern thinking, which revolves largely around Descartes' famous claim, 'I think, therefore I am'. For Descartes, my identity is buried somewhere in my mind, quite separate from my body. As Brock concludes, 'Descartes got it right in claiming that the soul touches the body at a particular point, but wrong in locating it in the pineal gland. Jesus looks further south, much nearer the waist, as the place where the "I" is decided and the "soul" is seated.'

Jesus, then, does not try to conceive the neighbour, the 'other' as someone 'out there' to whom we owe empathy. The love to which he calls the lawyer (and everyone else) arises from a self-hood understood not as an isolated, free-floating 'I', but as an embodied someone whose bowels react to someone else in distress. A person-in-relation-to-the-other, whose own wellbeing is rooted in that of the other, to the extent that one feels it viscerally, physically, in one's gut. I do not coldly rationalise in advance a just and proper way of acting towards another. I-and-the-other are already bound together, such that I already feel their distress as my distress. For the Good Samaritan, there is no 'I' who feels a duty to a subsequent external 'he.' The Good Samaritan sees the distress of *another,* and virtually shits *himself*. The bowels of the righteous are linked to the welfare of the victim.

The priest and the Levite do not react like this. But let's be clear. This is not to say that *every* priest and *every* Levite is destined to cross the road from those in distress. Rather, that it is possible to be (and to feel oneself to be) a good person – in any culture, we might add. The moment we shake our heads at those who cross the road from distress – we have already become them. The spirit that enables us to *condemn* them rather than *see ourselves in* them, is that same spirit that diverts our path from truly facing the other.

What matters is not whether *they* cross the road, but whether *we* do. Nor are we in a position to perceive whether we have crossed the road from human distress. That insight belongs to the person lying half-dead in the gutter. What matters in this story is their perspective on us. Otherwise, the modern reader *presupposes a mutual familiarity with the victim that they simply do not share.*

THE INVISIBLE WOMAN

Jesus had many women amongst his followers, some of whom helped to fund his movement from the earliest days. For women to abandon their communities to follow a travelling rabbi was unheard of, largely because their place in society was rooted in a complex set of family relations. By following Jesus, these women abandoned their old kinship ties (on which their entire personhood depended) and committed themselves to a new kinship group – the followers of Jesus. The way he related to women is exemplified perfectly in his interaction with the female unperson he encountered at the home of a leading Pharisee.

Then one of the Pharisees invited Jesus to dine with him; he went to the Pharisee's house and reclined at table.

Now there was a certain woman in the town known to be a sinner. When she learned that Jesus was dining in the Pharisee's house, she got an alabaster flask of perfume, and went and stood crying at his feet. Her tears bathed his feet, and with the hair of her head she wiped them dry; she kissed them and anointed them with the perfume.

The Pharisee hosting him watched all this and thought to himself, 'If this man were really a prophet, he would know who she is and what sort of a woman is touching him – seeing that she is a sinner.'

But Jesus spoke up to him, 'Simon, I have something to say to you.'

'Then say it, teacher!' he replied.

'There was a moneylender with two debtors. One owed him five hundred pieces of silver, the other fifty. Since they could not pay it

back, he graciously cancelled both debts. Now which of them should love him more?' Simon replied, 'I take it, the one with the greater debt cancellation.' Jesus said to him, 'You have judged rightly!'

Then, turning to the woman, he said to Simon, 'Do you see this woman? I came into your house, and you offered me no water for my feet; yet she has bathed my feet with her tears and wiped them dry with her hair. You have me no kiss of welcome; yet since I arrived, she has not stopped kissing my feet. You did not freshen my face with oil, yet she has anointed my feet, and with perfume. This is why I'm telling you that her sins, though there are plenty of them, have been forgiven, seeing that she has loved greatly. But the one who is forgiven little, expresses little love. Then Jesus said to her, 'Your sins are forgiven.'

The guests dining with him began to ask themselves, 'Who is this who even forgives sins?' Again, he said to the woman, 'Your loyalty has liberated you. Go in peace.'

(Luke 7:36-50)

Like many parents, I have spent countless hours driving teenagers to and from social gatherings. During one such journey on a dark and wintry evening, we had a quiet but confident female teenage passenger in a car otherwise full of males. And by jingo – into this densely packed confined space, she burbled her bowels and thus released a hideous cocktail of biochemical exhaust fumes with catastrophic putridity. The vapour was an immensely high concentrate of exothermic pollutants that left all but the culprit gasping for oxygen. Instantly, the vehicle filled with shrieks of agonised protest, laboured breathing, gagging sounds, loud accusations and a spirit of helpless despair. All windows opened and the sudden influx of cold night air amplified the angry complaints. In the midst of the howling and windswept chaos, there she sat – serene and satisfied, not remotely embarrassed. Once the smoke had cleared and the windows were back up, I asked her, 'Do you always enjoy it when you fart?' Without hesitation, she answered calmly and deliberately, 'It depends what comes with it'. The car collapsed into laughter, as the boys tried not to imagine what excretal terrors might indeed come with an eruption of carnivorous anal perfumes. As lungs slowly returned to normal functionality, one of them then asked how a girl so small and sweet could produce such a degree of aromatic disgust. Her reply was dismissive and expressionless: 'This girl can!'

Within the context of its day, Jesus' demand for gender equality is implicit but radical and dangerously progressive. The story of the altercation at Simon's house demonstrates how a woman who has attracted everyone's attention on account of the smell she produced (costly perfume), nevertheless remains invisible to them. Despite lacking any social status, the nameless woman achieves a status before God that leaves her outranking the most privileged figures present.

The fact that Jesus had been denied the basic courtesies of good hospitality reveals that he had been invited to the meal in order to be shamed by his host. In Jesus' simple, straightforward criticism of Simon, he moves beyond the petty provocations of the Pharisee and bulldozes through the entire honour/shame hierarchy that had ideologically conquered the nation. Jesus did not criticise Simon for breaking the moral norms of good behaviour, but for complying with them. It was perfectly acceptable, after all, for a social superior to shame his inferiors in order to remind them of their proper place in the world. In this case however, the host's pretensions of moral superiority exploded space-shuttle style and Simon's reputation crashed down to earth as shattered debris. Conversely, Jesus did not praise the woman for her sins, but for transgressing unjust social habits. Adding insult to injury Jesus declares her sins forgiven. As explained above, such a declaration is not an individualistic pronouncement of ethical shitlessness. It is rather the recognition that this woman has entered into a new era, a new way of being Israel, the new nation Jesus is building around himself. In this restructured society, her well-attested shame-worthy failings of the past are not counted against her and she is honoured in the *sight* of all.

Central to the entire exchange is Jesus' question, 'do you *see* this woman?' In the Israel of Simon, this woman – despite being notorious – remained invisible as a person. In the Israel Jesus sought to usher in, this low-status, nameless female sinner becomes visible to all – an example of the liberty she had won on account of her loyalty/faithfulness/trust. The pan-dimensional liberty Jesus initiated embraced invisible low-status women like her and demoted the high-status gammon-headed guardians of privilege.

In light of all this, Jesus was not a feminist, but his entire campaign would achieve what many modern feminists seek. Angela Y. Davis is one modern example of a campaigner whose wider concerns for social justice address the legitimate priorities of progressive feminism along the way. Davis is careful, nevertheless, to distinguish herself from those who promote what she deems 'glass-ceiling feminism', that is – a feminism that fights for its place within the existing socio-economic structures and therefore fails to *see* the women crushed beneath the weight of its own single-track ambition.

In Simon's company, the glass-ceiling feminist will demand the right to inflict on her social inferiors, as much privileged oppression as her vicious male counterparts. This particular strand of feminism that unwittingly privileges the ambitions of wealthy women to the detriment of the world's poorest women, is the quest for equal access to the highest echelons of debilitating systemic inequality. Toxic masculinity with a female face and a 'This Girl Can' badge, remains toxic. For Davis, this only buttresses the plight of the poorest women – fuelling systems of oppression (by unselfconscious endorsement) whilst heralding itself as a great moral breakthrough (achieving equality of outcome). Like Davis, Jesus is infuriated by the social conventions that allow the privileged and powerful to oppress the poverty-stricken and powerless. The ethnicity, the nationality, *and* the gender of unpersons are no barrier to the liberty Jesus is unleashing across Israel.

In sum, glass-ceiling feminism seeks minor tweaks to an unjust system but leaves the apparatus of abuse untouched. In contrast, Jesus levels his polemical wrath at the ideological apparatus that allows women to be abused, poverty to be ignored, refugees to be detested, widows and orphans to be neglected and wealth to be transferred up, up and away from unpersons. Jesus of Nazareth is not interested in breaking glass ceilings because he demolishes the entire structures into which those ceilings are built. The feminism of Jesus was radical for his day and ours, in accordance with the strand of Davis' radical feminism but at odds with the knee-jerk girl-power feminism created by late-stage capitalism.

This loudest demands for women's rights today might, after all, be encapsulated in the fridge-magnet feminism of the meme, 'This Girl Can.' The last business I saw to make use of this phrase was a private, fee-paying girl's school in central Cambridge. Fees for each student at this school will cost the bill-payer precisely 75% of the average UK worker's take-home pay. No wonder This [particular] Girl Can. By such a standard, however, the vast majority of girls cannot. The only reason This Girl Can is that a very wealthy person is paying her bill. Let me be clear, I am not and absolutely not objecting to the existence of private schools. Not at all. It is important, nevertheless, to note that in this context, the words, 'This Girl Can', actually mean, 'By giving us truckloads of cash, you very wealthy people are also very virtuous people.' Most parents who see this advert, of course, will have no access to truckloads of cash and as such must quietly accept that they are somewhat lacking in virtue. Feminism may well be a virtue, but *it depends what comes with it.*

THE SERMON ON THE MOUNT

Jesus did not preach sermons. He delivered prophecies, or at least, prophetic insight on the plight of his Galilean contemporaries. Many of the sayings attributed him did not originate with Jesus at all. Instead, Jesus takes popular sayings and radicalises them. The *Golden Rule* for instance ('do as you would be done to') is a common saying that Jesus takes and applies to loving one's enemies – namely, Roman oppressors. The counsel he offers to the crowds takes well-used pop-wisdom and radicalises it, showing how the expectations of Jewish liberation can be fulfilled in profoundly unexpected ways.

> *You have heard that it was said, 'Eye for eye, and tooth for tooth.' But I tell you, do not resist an evil person. If anyone smacks you on the right cheek, turn to them the other cheek also ... If anyone forces you to go one mile, go with them two miles. Give to the one who asks of you, and do not turn away from the one who wants to borrow from you.*
> *(Mt 5:38-42)*

At moments of national crisis, modern westerners rush to stockpile toilet-paper. During the 2020 pandemic, some manufacturers reported increased sales of 700 percent. The fact that societal panic defaulted straight to the anus rather than the stomach, the skin or the teeth (pasta, soap and toothpaste were less prone to increases in demand), reveals something important about modern humanity. We are obsessively worried about our shit. For this reason, we are anxious about our ease of access to toilet roll. In fact, more affluent Anglo-Saxons are abandoning dry toilet paper in favour of wet-wipes. One expert provides the following evidence for the necessity of this extravagant move:

> Here's proof on why people should have baby wipes. Get some chocolate, wipe it on a wooden floor, and then try to get it up with some dry towels. You're going to get chocolate in the cracks. That's why you gotta get them baby wipes. (*will.i.am*)

Maybe this is correct. Treating your body's most sensitive areas to the scented luxury of disposable moist wipes may seem highly commendable. But to many, you would only want your arse this clean if it's where you keep your own head. To many others, a baby wipe stained with Will.i.am's chocolate fudge-drop cannot be flushed down a toilet in any case, because the wipes do not break down in water and often cause difficulty further down the line.

In Jesus' day, the Romans used a sponge on a stick, soaked in vinegar. They called this a 'xylospongium', and it may be no coincidence that vinegar on a sponge-stick was mockingly shoved in Jesus' face as he was strung up on the cross. Unbeknown to the Romans, the sponge – especially when used in public latrines – could also spread infection and disease from one stoic blowhole to another.

The hygiene of Jewish culture has withstood the test of time far better. Jewish folk would use pebbles, leaves and old pottery to clean excretal remains from their hind quarters (*Shabbat* 81a, 82a, *Yevamont* 59b). Although using broken pottery as a wiping implement may sound like a potential act of anal self-harm, some today will remember the crisp, beige grease-proof toilet paper from the school restrooms of their childhood. These malevolent sheets of paperised-cruelty crumpled themselves around your hand into a deadly multi-spiked torture device no sane person would ever place within wiping distance their unprotected poo-chute. For many, it will come as no surprise that populations accustomed to such self-administered anal sandpapering could vote for Trump or Brexit.

In order to minimise the possibility of unintended faecal spread, many pre-toilet societies developed the convention of using the left hand to conduct toiletry affairs and the right hand for eating, working, greeting etc. (It may well be for this reason that in such cultures, left-handed folk were considered 'sinister' – i.e., they would instinctively use the same hand to greet you as they had just been using to dispose of broken fragments of pottery-scoopage). Jewish culture was no different in this regard, a key consideration when hearing Jesus' instruction to 'turn the other cheek'.

Traditionally, when we hear the instruction to 'turn the other cheek', we tend to regard this as inviting malicious people who have walked all over you, to walk all over you a little bit more. In other words, an act of pointless or masochistic stupidity. In the context of Jesus' day, those who do the walking are likely to be representatives of Roman power. In the context of Matthew's Gospel from which these words are drawn, the instruction forms part of the so-called 'Sermon on the Mount' (Matthew 5:1-7:28). In reality, however, Jesus never preached a sermon.

Anyone who has ever heard a 'sermon' will realise – presuming their brain is engaged – that it bears no resemblance to the 'Sermon on the Mount.' A sermon, much like contemporary mainstream op-ed journalism, is surely the practice in which those with an over-inflated sense of their own opinion appeal to iron age mythologies to deliver patronising morality monologues to the unenlightened and gullible masses. (Except for *my* sermons, of course, which are glorious exceptions to this rule. As are those of all other preachers – in their own minds). Jesus simply did not do this. When he spoke in the synagogues the atmosphere was more like a debating chamber than a preaching house. And when he delivered extended monologues, they were not sermons. They were prophecies. That is, they were a means of speaking truth to / about power, a highly dangerous move when executed from a position of powerlessness.

The prophecy he delivered offered a downtrodden and beleaguered people a powerful means of passive resistance. The Romans were hated oppressors (from whom you might want to exact revenge – as many Jewish people did a generation later). They imposed humiliating regulations designed to keep conquered people feeling in their bowels that they were conquered. They could commandeer the services of peasants, compelling these unpersons to assist the very oppressors who caused their suffering. These are the precise concerns addressed in turn within the passage cited above.

'An eye for an eye' was the Jewish wisdom of limiting the revenge you might wish to exact from someone who has hurt you. But Jesus counsels against exacting any payback at all from those nasty Romans. Instead, he counsels defiance by over-compliance. If a Roman 'smacks you on the right cheek' of what is presumably the face, he will be using the back of his right hand (since his left hand was reserved for self-administered anal sponging). A slap with the back of the hand is how they would strike inferiors. But by 'turning the other cheek' the unperson invites the Roman to slap them again, but this time using the palm of their right hand. This is how Romans would strike their social equals. As Walter Wink pointed out, Jesus' plea was an ingenious call to passive resistance. Similarly, the instruction to carry a Roman's pack (a soldier could compel local unpersons to carry their load for one mile), is greeted with over-compliance. By carrying the oppressor's pack for two miles instead of one, then Jewish people would walk the entirety of the two-mile journey in obedience to their gracious God, not in obedience to a pagan dictate.

On reading the 'Sermon on the Mount', most Anglo-Saxon readers will take it as Jesus' instructions to 'us' – that we should be nice to others, love our enemies, do good to nasty people etc. But for a more faithful interpretation of the text, we must also see ourselves as the powerful occupying force, the oppressor, the hated Roman. What if you and I are the very 'enemy' to whom Jesus calls his hearers to show restraint, compassion, love, and non-violent resistance? Given our location in world history, that should be the position we occupy in the text. We are the enemy, no matter how piously or loudly we bleat, 'not in my name'. We are the nation that drops a bomb every twelve seconds, killing hundreds of people every day, around 2 percent of whom were actual targets. We are the nation exempted – on account of our powerful history – from being charged with the war crimes we commit. We are the nation destroying the democracy of less powerful nations when those nations go rogue by dropping the dollar, becoming socialist, and sitting on oil reserves. And should you seek to resist us, or reveal our war crimes, or tell the truth about our actions, we will do what the Romans did to Jesus: we will take a sponge full of vinegarised faecal liquid, shove it on a stick and wave it mockingly in the face of your suffering.

To turn Jesus' courageous voice from the margins, into a 'sermon' about 'doing good' is to turn the biblical text into a sheet of moral toilet paper and use it to wipe the ethical excrement away from the pious back-pipe of my bad conscience.

Jesus was a prophet, not a preacher.

CALLING SINNERS

Jesus spent a lot of time with 'sinners', that is – people unable to meet the strict requirements not only of Jewish religious law, but of the legalistic conventions that had built up around that law. Many were simply too submerged in poverty and labour to comply with all law and convention. Others, however, looked down upon 'sinners'. Again and again, Jesus exposes how the very act of dismissing someone as a 'sinner' reveals one's own sinfulness. It is a message that is rarely well received.

> *As Jesus went along... he saw a man called Matthew, sitting at the customs toll. He said to him, 'Follow me.' And he got up and followed him. While he was sitting [for dinner] at his house, many tax collectors and sinners came and sat with Jesus and his disciples. When the Pharisees saw, they asked, 'Why is your teacher dining with tax collectors and sinners?' But when Jesus heard this, he said, 'It is not the healthy who need a medic, but the sick. So, go and learn what this means: "I desire mercy, not sacrifice," because I did not come to call on the righteous, but to call on sinners.'*
>
> *(Matthew 9:9-13)*

All modern toilet users will, at some point in their lives have encountered the dreadful phenomenon of 'the one that will not go down'. That is, a particularly virulent defecation with the consistency of redwood bark and the atomic weight of uranium. Having once splashed down – it has decided of its own volition, to stay put no matter what. The toilet user then faces a daunting challenge. After a failed first flush, if the toilet is within earshot of anyone else, you know that you have only one chance to get this right. More than two flushes and they will be alerted to the fact that you are locked in mortal combat with a former component of your own body that has broken free and developed a will of its own. What can mortals do against such a stubborn behemoth? Firstly, patience is imperative – you must wait for the tank to refill before going in for round 2, otherwise you will flush before the toilet has reloaded its godly ammunition. Stay calm: if your faecal foe has survived the flushing power of a full tank, then a second premature attempt with lessened force is already doomed to failure. Secondly, the toilet brush must be weaponised, in order to dismember, decapitate and disintegrate your opponent. Thirdly, you may need to look around for some form of receptacle that can hold water. If you find one, quietly fill this as far as possible using the sink and pour it quickly into the pan immediately after beginning the second flush – thus increasing the fluvial force to tsunamic levels. No excretal titan can endure this threefold hydraulic onslaught. Your unwanted log will be out of sight and out of mind. Sadly, the story does not end there.

While you are busy washing your hands like Pontius Pilate, your shit – regardless of how far it travels from your consciousness – still exists. Somewhere between your toilet and the sewer, excrement magically transforms from 'shit' into 'human waste', i.e., from something personally and intimately related to you, into a general and public matter that belongs to no one in particular. Should there be a sewage disaster and your poo resurface – it is no longer *your* subjective poo, but an objective, general problem 'out there' that impacts on everyone. Even if your turd is now floating proudly down the Thames, pierced with a toothpick carrying a miniature flag that bears your family crest, it is no longer deemed to have any direct relation to you. Modern sanitation has enabled you to disown it. You may indeed have washed your hands of it, but there it floats.

This is precisely how so-called 'sin' works in the New Testament. Most Christians regard sin solely as something *I* do, some form of subjective, personal wrongdoing that I – as an individual – commit. Hence, sinners are people who do terrible things (sins of commission), or who fail to do 'the right thing' (sins of omission). Either way – sin is an act of wrongdoing for which individuals are culpable. It enables those deemed righteous to point the finger at those deemed guilty. Such finger-pointing, however, is – in biblical terms – satanic. The satan, in Hebrew thought, is a legal metaphor denoting the council for the prosecution: the accuser, the pious and judgemental finger-pointer. Why should pointing out the wrongdoing of another be regarded as an evil in itself? Usually, because it is done by those who are unwitting accomplices in sin. In Sunday-School language – when you point the finger at someone, there are three hidden fingers pointing back at you.

From a secular perspective, sin is likewise often perceived as personal, individual wrongdoing – usually, an offence against a non-existent iron-age divinity whose irritating ghost still lurks in the shadows of modernity and in the minds of those who have never learned to think. It is personal and private, and if I don't believe in iron-age fairy tales why should it bother me remotely? The answer is simple: because it is 'remotely' that it bothers everyone, a bit like the shit you have deposited in the collective monstrosity called 'human waste'. No matter the lengths to which you may go to distance yourself from your own shit – there it floats.

Sanitation is profoundly underappreciated as a modern phenomenon – especially as it reveals how modernist ideology functions. It allows us to view the shitfulness of acts in which we have been complicit, as something 'remote', out there, nothing to do with us. This is exactly how sin functions – at least sin as conceived in the bible.

Naturally, we might look at the world's great evils and assume they have nothing to do with us: the political parties who – for the sake of clinging to power – make themselves beholden to corporate funders rather than to the voting publics they claim to represent; the media machines, bankrolled by those same corporate interests, that impose invisible regimes of truth designed to enforce either obedience or despair; the corporate takeover of our academic institutions that reduce once great universities to intellectual sausage factories where graduates subconsciously learn to comply rather than to question; the identity politics that gives my subculture a monopoly on truth and justice, cleverly designed to make me hate the very people with whom I might once have found productive solidarity; the social-media platforms that divert the attention of the masses into the confines of trivia, opinion, fashion and mutual separation, thus undetectably transforming people into products on sale to advertisers; the advertising industry that tells me I am not worthy unless I spend money I don't have on things I don't need; the construction of moralities that keep me focussed on symptoms rather than causes, that train me to cheer at the condemnation of truth-telling whistle-blowers who unmask this as our true state; the ideology that tells me I am a free-thinking, independent, justice-loving model of sensible demeanour, whilst ensuring that I remain a conformist sock-puppet for the corporate interests that grind the humanity out of the human condition.

The list could go on and on, of course, but these are the forces at work in our world that the New Testament regards as 'sin'. From a biblical perspective, individual sinners are simply those who are helplessly (and often unselfconsciously) implicated within these structures. An intimate part of us, in other words, is still floating through the sewers of late modernity – we are crucial contributors to all the shit in circulation.

What then, did it mean for Jesus to spend time with sinners? His response to those who criticized him was to claim that he came not for the healthy but for the sick, not for the righteous but for sinners. His followers, you might recall, were 'the shit of the earth'. Jesus then turns to his supposedly sin-free accusers, implying that their very accusation could be deemed the worst kind of 'sin' (accusations are satanic, after all). Here, I cannot help but recall how Dominique Laporte who, in his magnificent *History of Shit*, concludes his reflection on humanity's pride at its newly developed sanitation technology: 'By hoisting himself to the top of the hierarchical scale of creation, especially with regard to his 'excreta,' man is revealed in his earthiness as eternally, hopelessly *soiled*.' In other words, we are at our shittiest when we marvel at or own shitlessness.

Jesus' conclusion seems to be that everyone is somehow complicit in the injustices that plague our world – and the real question is how conscious his hearers really are of their true predicament. Most people regard a sinner as that identifiable victim who just can't rid themselves of their own dreadful turd. In contrast, Jesus has a knack of drawing the attention of his hearers to the turd that has parted company with their consciousness, no matter how remote it might now seem, re-uniting the moral hygienists with their own faecal produce. This was not in order to condemn them, but to reveal their true place in 'the hierarchical scale of creation'.

IV

The Road to Jerusalem

Jesus' activities in Galilee eventually came to the attention of Herod Antipas, at which point Jesus quits the region and begins his fateful journey to Jerusalem. The emphasis shifts from action towards proclamation. His message about 'the Kingdom of God' is a promise about the regime change he will soon trigger. As his reputation grows, he confronts opponents and enemies of ever greater status. Heading south through Samaria, then the towns and villages of Judea, his campaign gathers momentum.

THE LORD'S PRAYER

Different strands of first century Palestinian Judaism would often treasure a prayer that characterised the nature of their communal identity. This was something similar to a modern mission statement, though it was directed at God and embraced every dimension of the human life offering that prayer. Henry VIII helpfully improved Jesus' first attempt at putting together such an entreaty, thus transforming the Messiah's desperate plea into 'the Lord's Prayer'. Jesus did not sit his disciples in kindergarten rows, and preface his words with 'hands together, eyes closed' (practices derived from medieval supplicants grovelling to their feudal lords). This was a prayer that threatened the wellbeing of anyone who dared to utter it.

When he was praying in a particular place, it happened that – when he stopped – one of his disciples said to him, 'Lord, teach us to pray, just as John taught his followers.'

He said to them, 'Whenever you pray, say:
Father, Let your name be made holy,
Let your kingdom come,
Each day, give us our bread for the day,
Forgive us our sins,
Because we also forgive everyone indebted to us,
And do not bring us into a test.'
(Luke 11:1-4)

I read once about the solidarity a teacher attempted to show for one of his reception year students. At an age when farts have recently become funny in others, but embarrassing for oneself, a five-year-old girl in the class accidentally farted and became a class-wide object of ridicule. In a moment of compassion-fuelled solidarity, the teacher attempted to outperform the girl's mid-range bottom burp. Unusually, the teacher did indeed manage to summon up a demonic pocket of air from his innards, flexed his rectal muscles and forced the gas out through his turd-cutter. At first this felt like a success. Unfortunately, what had been intended as a loud trumpet call to laugh at him (thus deflecting ridicule away from his young student), instead manifested itself with malevolent silence. What the fart lacked in volume, it made up for in nasal toxicity. As a middle-aged man with poor dietary habits, the sulphuric brutality of his vapour was a veritable abomination. Since it arrived silently in the classroom, the other children assumed that the putrid fumes had emanated from the innocent child who was already mortally embarrassed. *What began as a self-less attempt at solidarity, not only failed to alleviate, but significantly worsened the suffering.*

Prayers in first century lower Galilee, were not shopping lists presented to an imaginary deity in the hope that he would supernaturally adjust the complex web of cosmic coincidence and human interaction to favour you and your loved ones. Instead, they positioned you in relation to others, to the universe, and to the God who runs everything. The prayer that Jesus taught his disciples – often known as 'the Lord's Prayer' – portrays a God in radical solidarity with humanity, and humanity in radical solidarity with one another.

Although it addresses God in patriarchal terms, in reality it short-circuited the entire patriarchal structure of the universe. From the marble corridors of Rome to the flea ridden hovels of the provinces – the role and rights of fathers were enshrined in law. The ultimate human super-father was the emperor – himself, descended from the gods, an earthly representative of Jupiter – a Latinised version of the Greek, 'Zeus-Pater' (Father Zeus). Fatherly authority dominated daily life from the greatest to the least. By addressing Israel's God as 'Father' – Jesus short-circuits the entire structure of imperial patriarchy. Jesus authorizes and exhorts his followers to go straight to the top. Have you been robbed of your lands, burdened with unjust tax, underpaid for your labour, mistreated by your master? Where do you find justice? From the head of your own household, from your patrons, the patrons of your city or province? In other words, do you expect to find remedy for injustice from those who inflicted it upon you in the first place? If you want justice – so the logic of the prayer runs – you need not be solely dependent on an earthly mediator. You go straight, directly to Israel's God who is in such radical solidarity with you that you can address him as 'Father'.

This is the non-imperial character whose kingly authority you acknowledge – and for whose kingdom you long. ('Let your kingdom come' is a dangerous cry for regime change). At the centre of the prayer, however, is the most radical demand for solidarity. The traditional language ('give *us* this day, our daily bread') contains the most abused 'us' in the history of western literature. This is a prayer that can only be made alongside/with/as those in poverty. The moment we pray FOR them, we are in the realm of selfie-stick solidarity: distancing ourselves from suffering – but trying to con God into thinking *we* care for *them*. The 'Lord's Prayer' is a boomerang that places responsibility for real life hunger back into the hands that are closed together in prayer.

The same dynamic of solidarity relates to the notion of debt cancellation. The quest for forgiveness of sins, is not to have one's moral slate cleaned because you've just been caught pants-down in the presence of a supernatural mind-reading judge who's just waiting for an opportunity to inflict eternal torment for minor infractions of an impossible-to-keep religious law book. Far from it – countless inhabitants of Galilee were kept deliberately on the brink of poverty, and often lived in debt to others. The prayer is a reminder that you don't get to have a clean slate with God, if you are benefitting from the poverty of others. The economic horrors that plagued Judea and Galilee would soon result in growing economic unrest, violent protest, armed resistance and catastrophe. Three Roman legions would soon descend on the province and crush this entire people, almost out of existence. This military atrocity was the 'test' ('temptation' is a terrible, individualised, depoliticised translation of the same word). Jesus wants his followers to avoid this test.

The historical context of the prayer is, of course, swept beneath the carpet of mainstream Christianity. Modern westerners pray FOR 'the poor', without having to be contaminated by them. Even referring to them as 'the poor' can subconsciously label this people as being pre-destined to a horrible life. When you see poverty up close, its ravages become horribly specific – and of course, have the capacity to effect bowel movements that lead to real action. But to pray the Lord's prayer today requires no godly stirring in the large intestine. Just a patronising nod, a smug sympathy, and – occasionally – a pious flicking of change in their general direction (usually by clicking or swiping in response to a charity appeal).

To pray the Lord's Prayer well, however, requires that you re-examine your place in the world and by implication your relation to structures that maintain unnecessary poverty. Your entire life can unravel when you ask those questions. Screw that. Instead, I will pray FOR the poor and leave all the mess (of which I am an unwitting beneficiary) in God's hands. 'Our Father. Poor people are your problem, not mine. But please remember I do care for them – if only you cared for them a little more, everything would be fine. Amen.' Fake solidarity, endorsing by inaction structures that worsen their plight, all in God's name. Behold: *The Lord's prayer began as a self-less attempt at solidarity, and today not only fails to alleviate, but significantly worsens the suffering of others.*

Rather than simply ride the bandwagon of religion-bashing (they're all a bunch of pious hypocrites), it is worth asking to what extent the moral guardians of self-proclaimed secular liberalism engage in the same brand of hypocrisy. Where policing the language and opinions of our politically incorrect peers feels courageous, because we are too cowardly to meet with the actual people on whose behalf we claim to speak. Where tolerating people serves as a substitute for listening to them in real life. Where we parade our virtue and register our righteous indignation online – because we would never dare dirty our hands or waste our time with 'the shit of the earth' (see above).

Whether we pray the Lord's prayer, or revel in our progressive credentials, it is always worth asking ourselves whether all we are doing is silently filling the heavens or the internet with a toxic wave of dastardly malodorous poo-vapour.

THE WHEAT AND THE TARES

En route to Jerusalem, Jesus spends a lot of time communicating in parables. The picture language of these stories is often taken literally and stitched together to construct a triple-decker universe with heaven at the top, hell at the bottom, and earth sandwiched between them like pâté. A key component of the parables cited here is the presence of angels – widely assumed to be supernatural figures who flutter out of a perfume commercial to execute merciless eternal judgement on mortals, usually for the crime of being mortal. This is how the message of Jesus' parables are frequently but ingeniously interpreted into their exact opposite.

> *So just as the tares are gathered up and burned with fire, so shall it be at the end of the era. The Son of Man will send his angels, and they will gather out of His kingdom all stumbling blocks, and those who commit lawlessness, and will throw them into the furnace of fire; in that place there will be weeping and gnashing of teeth. Then the righteous will shine forth as the sun in the kingdom of their Father. He who has ears, let him hear... Again, the kingdom of heaven is like a dragnet cast into the sea, and gathering fish of every kind; and when it was filled, they drew it up on the beach; and they sat down and gathered the good fish into containers, but the bad they threw away. So it will be at the end of the era; the angels will come and take out the wicked from among the righteous, and will throw them into the furnace of fire; in that place there will be weeping and gnashing of teeth.*
>
> *(Matthew 13: 40-43; 47-50 NASB)*

This passage could have been written by the collective mental health catastrophe that is Westboro Baptist Church. Angels, here, are pictured as the executors of a wrathful, vengeful God inflicting cosmic levels of abuse on wicked, law-breaking mortals who had failed to maintain impossibly high moral standards. Well. Not quite. A text without a context is a con. Jesus would be horrified at how Christians inflicted with obsessive compulsive literalism have twisted his prophecy. Jesus, whatever else he might have been, was a Hebrew prophet, who spoke in prophetic language and with prophetic urgency. He was warning his people about the end of an era, triggered by the destruction of Jerusalem's magnificent Temple.

Politically, this national disaster was a thoroughly avoidable atrocity. In the simplest (though perhaps crudest) terms, 'the righteous' (better translated, *those who embodied justice*) were those Jewish folk who avoided the militant xenophobia that dominated the build-up to the Jewish rebellion and Roman invasion of the late 60s – at least as the contemporary historian Josephus describes the war. The 'wicked' were the militant xenophobes who presumed God was on their side, and whose rebellion against Rome would lead inevitably to their own destruction. The 'angels' were the executors of divine judgement – i.e., the Roman soldiers who reduced the beautiful city of Jerusalem to a wasteland of smouldering debris. Tragically, the prophecy came true in the 70th year of the first century.

The fact that pagan soldiers might serve as unwitting messengers of Israel's God does not make them 'angels' in a moral sense. In that same period building up to the Jewish War, during a mass feast in the Temple, one of the Roman soldiers provoked a riot by pulling down his pants to show his ass to the worshippers. As Josephus reports the incident,

> *...when the multitude were come together to Jerusalem, to the feast of unleavened bread, and a Roman cohort stood over the cloisters of the temple, (for they always were armed and kept guard at the festivals, to prevent any innovation which the multitude thus gathered together might make), one of the soldiers pulled back his garment, and cowering down after an indecent manner, turned his breech to the Jews, and spake*

> *such words as you might expect upon such a posture. At this the whole multitude had indignation, and made a clamour to Cumanus, that he could punish the soldier... the violence with which they crowded to get out was so great, that they trod upon each other, and squeezed one another, till ten thousand of them were killed...*
>
> (Josephus, *Wars of the Jews* 2.11)

The first time I read this in its original Greek, it struck me only that the soldier had unveiled his arsehole and shouted insults through his face-hole. The incident has since been cited ad nauseam by comedians and tabloid journalists alike, claiming that the soldier in question farted, making it 'the fart that killed ten thousand people'. In reality, the soldier was probably positioned on the ramparts of the Antonia Fortress that overlooked the Temple – within sight of worshippers, but well beyond their earshot – even if he had pulled off the most voluminous rectal blastation in the history of vertebrates. (Especially, we must add, if this gargantuan volcano of flatus were to be heard above the noise of tens of thousands of pilgrims). In any case, that particular Roman soldier who triggered this disaster certainly did not behave like an angel.

An angel, in Ancient Greek, is simply a 'messenger' and messengers throughout the Bible have multiple roles. What most people imagine to be an angel is a spiritual being who appears to announce God's intent, enact his judgement, and administer his support. Such semi-divine figures do not play a major role through the course of Jesus' campaign. They announce the births of Jesus and John the Baptist, and they appear to assist Jesus after his ordeal in the 'Temptation in the Wilderness'. They then withdraw for the duration of Jesus' activities in Galilee and Judea. Only when Jesus experiences mortal fear as he nears his end, do they reappear to offer support, and later announce the resurrection to Jesus' followers.

The Bible as a whole has surprisingly little to say about angels – they feature only occasionally and at the margins of human experience and existence. Whilst they may appear in human form, they seem to be spiritual, non-physical beings – unconstrained by the frustrations and limitations of humble, physical human form. Angels, as the Bible portrays them, would not feel anything in their bowels, would not piss and shit (except, perhaps, into a Japanese toilet) and – if they were to fart – we might imagine that their gas could be bottled by Roja Parfum and sold at Harrods. Jesus, by stark contrast, was thoroughly human. Through and through he was the 'word made flesh', eternity cramming itself into mortality. Angels were non-physical, hovering instead somewhere above the gritty realities of earthly existence. This reality seems to be accentuated by their wardrobes – often dazzling raiment of purest white. Clean white clothes would be a rarity in ancient Palestine.

The phenomenon of white clothes itself highlights the non-human aspect of angelic being, unpolluted, unsullied, undefiled by any kind of impurity. It is hardly compatible with real human life. In the portacabin, for instance, it's a brave, brave man that wears pure white underpants. A safer choice of colour for undergarments would be coffee cream, yellowed grey, or – best of all – a mottled combination of soggy-brown, strangely-green and suspicious-red. Whilst underpants in these disaster-proof camouflage patterns are not currently available, they were once produced in the glorious form of 'paisley'. Many in my generation will recall the paisley-patterned y-fronts of their forefathers in the 1970s – a pragmatic option for a more sensible age. No longer. Nowadays, those who venture through their day wearing pure white underpants tread with self-conscious care. Every toilet visitation and gut-vapour exhalation – no matter how odourless or insignificant – becomes a potential moment of historic importance. And pure white underpants keep a more reliable permanent, in-erasable record of such activities than the NSA keeps on your internet activity.

Jesus did not wear the white clothes of uncontaminated purity. Jesus was polluted, infected with close interaction and relationship with undesirables, with sinners, with the shit of the earth. If he were a God in human form, then this is not a God who kept real people at arm's length, who concealed shit from his sight, and who protected his nasal passages from the toxic vapours of real life. He touched the untouchable, he allowed himself to be touched by those whose immorality was infectious, he washed the stinking feet of others and allowed his own feet to be washed with tears and perfume. He shat and he pissed, he hiccupped and he belched, he sweated and he farted. Jesus was no angel.

WOE TO PHARISEES

Pharisees were rightly regarded as heroic figures by much of the populace in Jesus' day. Their name is probably rooted in the Hebrew word, 'pharash' – which means to separate. Whilst there is no simple creed that can identify this movement, it is clear that Pharisees were profoundly concerned with moral and religious purity. They were 'separate' in that they sought to remain uncontaminated by any form of impurity. But traditionally, the Pharisaic movement, also cared deeply about people. This was why they had long commanded the respect of the people, why they had great influence with the people, and it was why powerful tyrants learned to exploit the Pharisees' respected status to serve their own purposes. It was on those exploited, unwittingly compromised wings of the Pharisaic movement that Jesus turned his rhetorical arsenal.

> *Once Jesus had spoken, a Pharisee invited him to dine with him. He went in and sat down.*
>
> *The Pharisee, as he watched, was shocked that [Jesus] did not first wash before the meal.*
>
> *The Lord said to him, 'Now you Pharisees clean the outside of the cup and the platter; but within you are full of greed and evil. You idiots! Did not the one who make the outside make the inside as well? So then, as far as what is inside is concerned, you should give alms. Then, lo and behold, everything would be clean for you. Unfortunately, you Pharisees are doomed: You pay voluntary tax on mint and rue, and every edible plant, but you ignore justice and the love of God. You Pharisees are*

doomed: You love the best seat in public meetings and the greetings in the marketplaces. You are doomed: You are like unseen tombs, which people walk over without realising.
(Luke 11:37-44)

I have three sons. On a warm summer evening years ago, before he was toilet trained, I noticed one of them squatting on the garden patio. It was a distinctive kind of squat-posture, the kind only ever adopted for one activity. When you're a toddler, the world is your potty. Given that he was already mid-procedure, it would have been futile and indeed cruel to intervene, so I allowed events to run their natural course. From such a tiny body, the excretal product was disproportionately sizeable. The front end of the first brown cylinder had touched down on planet earth before the rear end had parted company with the brown star. This, in turn, required the poor boy to 'dismount' the faecal mass that his own body had delivered. Once he was stood clear, the turd stood proud – as perpendicular as a Saturn V rocket ready for lift-off. But my son's facial expression (profound concentration) and body language (preoccupation with the task at hand) revealed that this operation was far from complete.

Having repositioned himself, he repeated the process – the end product being a second tower of nut-brown profusion of exactly the same proportions as the first. The entire adventure must have virtually hollowed out his tiny frame. Again, he dismounted and repositioned himself, finishing the job by dropping a couple of minor boulders. Then he stood back to marvel at his achievement as though these twin towers ranked among the wonders of the world. The involuntary smile that followed was not relief, nor amusement, but sheer well-warranted pride. In defiance of gravity, his two towers cast long shadows over the patio, and it seemed a shame to dismantle and dispose of them.

In first century Judaism, the Pharisees were a political pressure group without power of their own, but whose concern was for the people of God to remain faithful to the Law of God. It was a concern shared by Jesus, though Jesus had a wildly different strategy to achieve that goal. Where Pharisees added extra legal regulations to clarify Moses' law, Jesus instead sought to awaken the spirit of God's law in the spirit of God's people.

The Pharisees have a terrible press in the New Testament. From the outset, it is important to note two key aspects of Jesus' interactions with Pharisees. Firstly, he profoundly disagreed with them. Secondly, he spent a lot of time arguing with them – implying that as a group he considered them worthy of his energy and attention. In fact, the Pharisees were the forerunners of the Jewish leaders today known as Rabbis. And as a former chief Rabbi once told me in an interview, the ferocity of debate and enmity between Jesus and the Pharisees might be deemed perfectly normal and healthy, and you could picture them 'going for a pint' afterwards.

This seems perfectly reasonable, since it is the kind of habit we might witness today between those with shared goals but alternative methods. Jesus cared deeply about the Pharisees and Jesus heavily criticized the Pharisees. They were widely perceived as champions of the people, seeking means of interpreting Jewish law so as to make it easier for common folk to comply. Many of the effects of Mosaic law, especially on the poorest people, could be deemed harsh and severe. For instance, one law demands that parents execute rebellious children (Dt 21:18-21), especially if they are going to shit on your patio. The Pharisaic tradition wrapped this command in so much interpretive red tape it could never have been applied. Pharisees cared about the poorest echelons of Israelite society. The fact that Jesus accused them of the exact opposite would have been shocking.

It would be the equivalent today of a leader attacking the Democratic Party for being undemocratic, unwittingly denying its own core principles and betraying the very people it has long since claimed to support (and growing numbers of progressives are voicing these very accusations). This is precisely the charge Jesus levels at the Pharisaic party. After all, Jesus' priority was those people widely deemed 'the shit of the earth' (St Paul's phrase), a 'basket of deplorables' (Clinton's phrase), and 'peasants with pitchforks' (Obama's – yes, Barak Obama's phrase). For many of Jesus' listeners, it would simply have been unthinkable that the Pharisees themselves, the traditional champions of the people, could be complicit in oppressing those people. After all, they retained the language and habits of piety (much like compromised political parties retain language of democracy, justice, fairness etc), i.e., cleaning the outside of the bowl and leaving the inside to decompose. The modern equivalent might be those for whom political correctness (using inoffensive language, policing the language of others, hating the right people etc) serves as pious substitute for listening seriously, carefully and directly to 'the shit of the earth.' As an institution Jesus charges the Pharisees with political correctness devoid of justice.

According to some scholars, we do not have reliable first-hand evidence written by any Pharisees. But this is not quite true. It is possible that the Jewish historian Josephus was a Pharisee (he certainly claimed to have been a Pharisee.). But the New Testament does contain many writings attributed to a former Pharisee, Saul of Tarsus. After his famous Damascus road conversion, he devoted himself to Christ and became Saint Paul the Apostle. Paul described himself as an uber-Pharisee, who was immensely proud of the righteousness he had achieved by Pharisaic means. In fact, it was to Paul that we owe the phrase, 'shit of the earth'. But Paul had more to say about shit. Reflecting on his own righteousness, he lists his credentials as a quintessential law-abiding Pharisee, whose conduct was faultless. His 'acquired status' (his Pharisaic lineage) and his 'attributed status' (his rigorous adherence to the law) stood like two magnificent towers, worthy and beautiful, wonders of the ancient world. But then, standing back and marvelling at his achievements, Paul proudly declares, 'I consider them shit' (Phil 3:8). He had taken to heart the words of Christ. Paul valued the magnificence of his own proud heritage on the one hand, and his faithful compliance with that heritage on the other, in precisely the same way that my son had valued his dual achievement on the garden patio.

FEAR OF THE PHARISEES

Once an opinion is settled into a person's mind, it is not easily changed. How easy is it for anyone to question their own ethical credentials if someone exposes their ethical blind spots? It takes an astronomical degree of confidence to re-examine the foundations of your own moral framework – and doubtless many Pharisees had precisely that confidence. Many, however, did not. Confidence is – above all else – the ability to confide, to face up to who you really are in relation to others and to the world. Confidence is the pre-condition for confession – i.e., to speak out the truth about who you really are. The vast majority of us who prefer to fake it (even to ourselves) are likely to experience Jesus' penetrating gaze as an ethical colonoscopy. No wonder people seem to move uncomfortably as they leave his presence.

> ... Even many leaders of the people trusted [Jesus], but *were refusing to confess this* for fear of the Pharisees (who might have expelled them from the synagogue). After all, they were more worried about their social status than their status before God.
>
> And Jesus shouted out, 'Whoever trusts me, does not trust me but the one who commissioned me.
>
> *Whoever* sees me, sees the one who commissioned me.
>
> I have come as Light into the world, so that everyone who trusts me will not remain in darkness.'
>
> *(John 12:42-46)*

In 1994 I worked for a scaffolding company, repairing an oil refinery that had recently exploded. The impact had obliterated the plant and taken out shop windows several miles away. The refinery itself was left as a burned-out wasteland of tangled steel, with a newly erected city comprised of portacabins to house hundreds of emergency repair workers. Everyone present was carefully trained to report instantly the smell of hydrogen sulphide (rotten egg odour) using a hotline number, since it might be an indication of another major hazard. In such a setting, the consequences of a gang of scaffolders taking their lunch break in a portacabin are predictable. On one occasion, the eggs I had enjoyed at breakfast several hours earlier triggered disturbing volcanic activity somewhere in the large magma chamber of my lower intestine. It was only a matter of time before a cloud of ash forced its way out of my dorsal conduit.

The cabin was lively and loud, comprised of rough workmen in yellow coats and blue overalls – innocently engaged in their daily routine of arguing and insulting, busily a-laughing and a-joking – just like the inhabitants of ancient Pompeii as Vesuvius quietly rumbled in the distance. They were oblivious to the human volcano perched on the blue plastic chair in the corner. The eruption was far from silent, but there was so much noise it went unheard. It could not go unnoticed. Howls of olfactory agony began to fill the lunch break, but my fellows were unaware of my guilt. There had been a direct link between my choice of protein-rich breakfast and the egg-flavoured calamity that had now overtaken the portacabin: since eggs contain sulphur-packed methionine, there was fear of a hydrogen sulphide leak. Not surprisingly, someone shouted 'call the f***ing hotline'. Others suggested making calls to various of the emergency services. And in these situations, there are always those who seek to protect their dainty nasal cavities by breathing in through their mouth rather than their nose. On this occasion it brought great personal satisfaction to hear one such attempt result in the half-choked splutter, 'Bloody hell! I can taste scrambled egg.' I considered making a public confession, but in a sense the chemical payload delivered through my colonic vent already constituted a confession, as I will now explain.

When most people think of confession, they automatically imagine owning up to terrible sins and godless crimes. Whilst this is sometimes the case, in Greek, to confess means nothing more than, 'to say the same thing'. To express with one's lips, that which lies in the inner recesses of one's being. In the passage cited above, for instance, some leaders were refusing to confess (to acknowledge publicly) their (inner, personal) trust in Jesus' message because they were afraid of the social and personal consequences.

The economist Stephanie Kelton tells the story of how a US congressman (Rev Emanuel Cleaver) was converted from a prevailing myth about how the US deficit worked, to an entirely and radically alternative economic model (Modern Monetary Theory - MMT) that promises a far brighter future for the American people.

She and her colleague, Warren Mosler, had visited his office to encourage him to support a change in US economic policy. Although at first he had been entirely sceptical, Kelton explains,

> [w]ith only a few minutes remaining in our hourlong scheduled meeting, it happened. The Copernican moment. I recognized it immediately. Mosler's words had clicked. It was the breakthrough we had hoped for. For the first time, the congressman was seeing the world through an MMT lens, and things had just come into focus. From that moment, his entire demeanour changed. His eyes widened. His posture became confident. And then he leaned forward, clasped his hands, looked Warren in the eye, and softly said, 'I can't say that.' (Kelton, *The Deficit Myth*, 2020)

Kelton understood that Cleaver was too much of a political realist to express publicly the truth to which he had been privately converted. In biblical terms, Rev Cleaver – as a 'leader of the people', could not summon up the courage to *confess*, to 'say the same thing' in public as he believed in private. After all, for Rev Cleaver to confess his newly acquired economic belief would be the equivalent of walking into congress, taking the floor, and farting straight into the microphone. Why?

As shown above, the world of modernity is a world structured around separating life into tidily distinct spheres of activity. Public and private, political and personal, science and religion, physical and spiritual etc. Life is like a pie chart with segments that do not overspill into one another. It is a worldview that promotes the practice of compartmentalising our lives. Rev Cleaver, for instance, was perfectly happy to separate the public from the private, and – as Kelton points out, the religious ('the truth shall set you free') from the political (political realism dictates that people won't welcome that truth). This enables the modernist to have different spheres of life, mutually distinct avenues of disjointed thought, making genuine confession impossible. How can you 'say the same thing' when a person is a concoction of non-overlapping segments, mutually exclusive compartments, distinctly separate fragments?

To confess, to 'say the same thing' well, is to enforce continuity through all elements of a person's life. It presupposes a degree of self-awareness, of integrity, of consistency through all the complex, overlapping, interweaving dimensions of your being. To confess is to transgress the boundaries of modernity. These boundaries can be like red tape that separates us from others and ultimately from ourselves. The voluntary move from private (individual, secret, personal) to public (in the sense of opening one's true self to another real person) can be a terrifying if liberating move.

This is a key dimension of the biblical phrase cited by Kelton that 'the truth shall set you free' (John 8:32). The Greek word for truth (a-letheia) refers to the pulling back the curtain surrounding something that had been hidden. It is a two-part word, like dis-closure, un-veiling, re-vealing. It involves the self as well as the other, the subject as well as the object. To engage truthfully is not simply to offer your assent to some form of cosmic correctness. It is rather to 'dis-close' the once-closed-self in order to encounter the universe more fully. It is for this reason that 'the truth shall set you free' – or translated differently, 'disclosure will liberate you.'

This brings us all the way back to confession. Part of the reason that people are offended, disgusted or amused by farting is that it transgresses treasured boundaries. What was once concealed is revealed, complete continuity between what is in a person's heart (or bowels) and what they speak through their face-holes (or arseholes). To be 'anally retentive' (in modern if not Freudian parlance) is to desire order over honesty, keeping one's mouth shut (like Rev Cleaver) and one's rectal muscles tight (preventing the truth from setting you free). To confess is to allow one's internal sulphur out into the world to bring whatever chaos it must.

THE YEAST OF THE PHARISEES

Jesus has, by now, amassed swelling crowds, and makes use of his platform to unburden himself of a major gripe with the Pharisaic party. It would be tempting, no doubt, for him to ingratiate himself with the crowds, to tell the crowds what they want to hear for the sake of his own popularity. Instead, he issues stark warnings about a hypocrisy that grips all humanity – even and especially those who might widely have been considered immune: Pharisees. Those like Jesus, who challenge rather than bow to public opinion, will soon find themselves demonised by the Public Relations industry. In Jesus day, that was an industry controlled largely by the Pharisees.

> *Meanwhile, when a crowd of many thousands had gathered, so that they were trampling on one another, Jesus began to speak first to his disciples, saying: 'Be on your guard against the yeast of the Pharisees, which is hypocrisy. There is nothing concealed that will not be disclosed, or hidden that will not be made known. What you have said in the dark will be heard in the daylight, and what you have whispered in the ear in the inner rooms will be proclaimed from the roofs.'*
> *(Luke 12:1-3)*

Benjamin Franklin once drafted a letter to the Royal Society requesting that research be committed to flatulence. In particular, to making human farts emit an aroma that is a pleasure to inhale, despite them having escaped the dorsal spigot via the poo-kissed lining of one's excretal duct. Whilst this request might well have been 'tongue in cheek' (in the present context, that's a mental image you may not wish to picture too literally), free-lance scientists have long-since sought to discover the secret of flatulence-flavouring. In Franklin's words, we might then 'fart proudly'. In 2018, for instance, one French genius claimed to have invented pills that achieve just that: natural concoctions that scent your intestinal gas with a variety of sweet aromas. Whilst his story was published in the *Daily Mail* and *Welsh News Online*, the research has never made it into *Science* or *Nature* magazines and probably remains something of a spoof.

In reality, the most effective means of transforming shit-vapour into perfume would presumably be via some kind of mechanical anal insert. When offensive gaseous chemicals prepare to burst out through one's abdominal wind-tunnel, they would be funnelled into the internal end of the insert, undergo a filtration process, and enter a miniature contraption containing neutralising agents. The final stage in the process would be a perfuming facility (possibly with changeable cartridges in a variety of scents). From there, the once-poisonous vapour would be ready to enter into polite society as a fragrant offering, thus making the world a safer and better place. The deluxe version of the anal insert might include a downloadable app, so that when the mechanism is activated it triggers digital devices within range to play an excerpt (of appropriate duration and volume) from Handel's *Hallelujah Chorus*.

However, whatever your body produces via the colonic insert – it would not be you. It would be something external to you. The scents you emit at those within nose-shot, would also not be you. The notion of something external to you, shaping how you would like to be perceived, is most fully described by the biblical notion of 'hypocrisy'.

When most of us think about hypocrisy we think of the symptom rather than the cause. The symptom is something along the lines of being guilty of what you condemn in others. But the roots of hypocrisy are something profoundly different. To be a hypocrite is to live your life in accordance with a body of rules, or ideals, or values to which you try to measure up. You esteem them so highly, in fact, that they are honoured above and beyond real-life, and remain external to you, either 'up there' somewhere as your highest aim – or 'down there' as principles or foundations, beneath your feet. In both cases – such values remain external. They become your own 'authoritative text' (regardless of whether they are solemnly written or subconsciously treasured), your own body of rights and wrongs (learned from your peers, your culture, or your religion). But 'values' remain separate to who you really are as a person, at a safe distance from the core of your human make-up. This is the normal standard of moral philosophy in the modern world. Principles, laws, values, duties, or morals 'out there', 'up there', removed from 'me' – and then you learn them, and subsequently apply them. All of these overarching laws remain at a safe distance from who I really am. If this is how morality functions – it is, by definition – hypocritical. It is a body of regulation, that you obey, you apply, you follow, you value, you treasure, you defend – but it is not you.

So much for morals. These are *mores,* i.e., rules, conventions, laws. Ethics, however, are something entirely different. Ethics concerns your *ethos,* the formation of your character, your experience, your interactions – and reaches into the core of your being. Jesus was far less concerned with obeying the rules of *morality* than he was with the shaping of a person's *ethos.* Once the ethos is well-attuned, morals are far less necessary. For Jesus, the ethos is formed by loving the 'other', and the kind of love to which he called his followers is precisely the subject matter of the Gospels. Saint Augustine famously summarised this dynamic with an exhortation of his own: 'Love, and do as you like.' In other words, 'allow your ethos to be forged by lovingly relating to the other, and your ethics will look after themselves (you won't need moral rules to please them).

The prophets of Hebrew Tradition recognised that many in Israel treated their Scriptures as a moral rather than an ethical code. That is, many people treated the Law or 'Torah' as a body of regulations external to who they were as people. For this reason, the prophet, Jeremiah longed for the day when the Torah would be inscribed into the core of their being. Relaying God's will for a new covenant, Jeremiah delivered God's word:

> *"This is the covenant that I will make with the House of Israel..." says the LORD: "I will put my law in their bowels and write it on their hearts" (Jer. 31:33).*

Once again, the God of Israel – and healthy human ethics – requires access to the human bowels. In this light, it may be noteworthy that the word 'rectitude' (the state of ethical-goodness) is derived from the same Latin word as 'rectum' (the upper arse-tunnel).

In the passage above, the Pharisees in question have received and bequeathed traditions that separate ethical action from the bowels. But as Jesus goes on to say, 'There is nothing concealed that will not be disclosed, or hidden that will not be made known.' In other words, whatever is at work in your bowels is going to work its way out whether you like it or not.

Allowing your bowels to trumpet your inner secrets is called 'confession'. Protecting your bowels from moral deliberation is called 'hypocrisy'. And this is by no means restricted to those deemed to have a religious disposition. Take xenophobia. Few people treasure xenophobia as a moral ideal or personal value. It tends to be the kind of anti-virtue that only exists as a derogatory accusation, never as a proud mark of self-identity. As such, avoiding xenophobia is the perfect example of a moral law.

Because it is an external law – for that very reason I am predisposed not to recognize my own xenophobia. Countless enlightened, intellectual, free-thinking, open-minded, tolerant, self-identifying-liberals – embody the most toxic xenophobic traits: Attributing xenophobia to *Daily Mail*-reading, *FoxNews*-watching, Brexit-voting, Trump-supporting, Flat-Earthing, misogynistic, racist right-wingers – I miss the irony that I actually know less than a handful of the millions of people I thus condemn. Labelling as 'xenophobic' people I would never dare to meet in real life (unless they are delivering my shopping, cutting my hair or fixing my car), reveals that xenophobia is my very own true status. That is the most insipid and dangerous form of xenophobia. It is also pure, unadulterated hypocrisy in the biblical sense: my moral ideals fiercely denounce xenophobia; my ethical character unwittingly treasures it.

Once you feel the reality of your own xenophobia in your own bowels, a different ethics can begin to emerge. Xenophobia, after all, is a human trait, an evolutionary product – a form of tribalism necessary for basic day-to-day functioning. We do not live our lives theoretically open and unafraid of everyone that is different to us – we simply cannot function that way unless not a single particular real-life person actually matters to us.

The moment you love, you fear – you fear losing something precious. The moment you fear, you are susceptible to hate – to hate those you perceive as a threat. The moment you hate, you are a xenophobe – no matter how passionately you reject the label. Those best qualified to assess my xenophobia – are the people on the receiving end of it. The very people whose real voice I am afraid to hear. No one is immune to any kind of xenophobia. Misogyny, racism, prejudice, closed-mindedness are all traits as quintessentially liberal as a de-caffeinated oat-milk flat-white. From a biblical perspective, 'all who say they have no sin deceive themselves'. What matters is rather, that you are enmeshed in the kinds of relationships that allow others to hold you to account when your xenophobia poisons the environment around you. That accountability reaches into the depths of your bowels.

Ethics is one thing. But values and principles, foundations and duties? These are anal inserts. When we begin tut-tutting and head-shaking, pointing the finger at political incorrectness, seething with anger that others don't share our values, the anal insert is activated. When we tolerate rather than listen to those who do not share our principles, when we look down on the inhabitants of 'flyover country', when we vent our contempt for the xenophobia of others – we should also be able to hear the Hallelujah Chorus.

SABBATH AND JUBILEE

Observing the Sabbath was one of the central identity markers of the Jewish people of Jesus' day. Sabbath comes from a Hebrew verb (*shavat*) that simply means 'stop', and everything stopped for Sabbath. For many, however, Sabbath had devolved into a religious law, set adrift from its origins. Jesus will remind his hearers of the radical foundations of the Sabbath tradition and this will get him into trouble with those who most treasured that tradition.

And he was teaching in one of the synagogues on the Sabbath. And look: a woman who had a spirit of sickness for eighteen years. She was bent double and could not straighten herself up.

Having seen her, Jesus beckoned her and said to her, 'Woman! You have been liberated from your sickness!' And he laid hands on her. And immediately she was straightened up and began glorifying God.

The leader of the synagogue, however, was exasperated because Jesus had healed on the Sabbath. He reacted and kept telling the crowd, 'There are six days on which it is necessary to work. So come on one these to get yourselves healed, and not on the day of the Sabbath.'

But the Lord replied to him, 'Hypocrites! Does not each one of you release his ox or donkey from the feeding trough and lead him to drink? But was it not inevitable that this woman, who is a daughter of Abraham, whom Satan had already bound for eighteen years, should be released from this chain on the day of the Sabbath?'

(Lk 13:10-16)

One of my earliest childhood memories is of my older sister, my younger brother and myself being aggressively whispered at by my slightly alarmed mother. We had been instructed to hide behind the sofa and make no noise. Crouched between the wall and the red fake-leather of our front room settee, we felt enough of her panic to comply. My brother, however, was only two or three years old at the time. It was a momentous day for him as the knocking began. The repeated pounding on the front door, then on the front window, then back on the door seemed endless. Then followed a short reprieve. And in that silence, from my brother's direction came a short, sweet bottom burp with a rising intonation that punctuated itself with a question mark. Was it safe to come out?

My brother was too young to realise that arse-wobbling gas leaks were hilarious – but when he saw the reaction of his older brother and sister, he caught on very quickly. While we were busy covering our mouths and chewing our sleeves lest we laugh out loud, our bodies were no doubt shaking frantically through the silence with suppressed hilarity. The eerie calm ended with a sudden loud hammering, this time from the back window where there was no net curtain to blur the caller's view. It made us all jump and as my brother jumped, he piped out a second round of bubble-and-squeak. It was agonizing for my sister and me whose restraint was already stretched to breaking point, and by now my brother had caught on. He joined us in our silent laughter. Furthermore, he was also young enough to release pockets of his fart-gas at will.

Thus, my little brother – with enormous self-amusement – learned how to blast his jubilaic horn. Somehow, we managed to keep our furious sniggers at low volume, but that red settee must have been shaking with the vibrations of our collective hysterics. The terrifying would-be intruder at the door, unbeknown to us, was a debt-collector, and was clearly oblivious to the historic drama that was unfolding under his very nose.

The woman in the Bible story above was debt in human form. She was not only 'bent double' but also unable to 'straighten herself' up. She is the physical manifestation of poverty, a word whose imagery is rooted in the description of the person who stoops/bends/shrinks (*ptosso* in Greek), who crouches (beneath oppression), who cowers (due to social dishonour), whose head hangs low (after losing a contest). People so inflicted as to be incapable of straightening themselves up and are located beneath the bottom rung of the honour-shame ladder of ancient Palestinian society. This woman stands out as a primary recipient of Jesus' message: she publicly embodies the physical traits of the poor for whom he has brought good news; she has been a metaphorical prisoner (of Satan); she needs to be set free. There is no mention of how her healing took place. Only that it was instantaneous, as was her praise.

The ruler of the synagogue was less enamoured with Jesus. But he was no petty legalist. A popular leader from out of town had come into his community, into his synagogue, and violated one of Israel's most precious commands: the Sabbath. By Jesus' day, all manner of regulations had built up around the Sabbath – the day of rest. And healing – according to tradition – constituted work. Jesus ignores the tradition and takes his coordinates only from Hebrew Scripture.

Whatever else Sabbath meant, historically it was designed to prevent the suffering caused by unfair distribution of wealth. It was a miniature version of the 'year of Jubilee' that took place every fiftieth year, a time when all debts were cancelled, debt-slaves were freed, the fields were left fallow, and families long separated by poverty were restored to their ancestral lands. This radical practice had been learned from other Mesopotamian cultures. Sumerian, Babylonian, and Persian rulers knew that the measure was sometimes necessary in order for them to continue to collect taxes, have their lands farmed, and protect themselves and their people from the formation of a permanent oligarchic class of ravenous creditors. The text of the Rosetta Stone – familiar to most as the famous key to deciphering Egyptian and hieroglyphics – is actually a decree of debt amnesty. However, where most cultures declared amnesties sporadically (often in times of war, famine or natural disaster), Jewish law demanded that they were issued regularly. Hence, every fiftieth year was declared a Sabbath of Sabbaths. It was called Jubilee because it was introduced by the sounding of the *Yabel* horn, the 'jubilaic' trumpet of a royal decree.

The weekly Sabbath celebration was not simply 'a day off' but a micro-celebration of that great Jubilee year, a regular reminder to the entire community that all are equal before God, and that if God writes off the debts of his people, then his own people ought not to be indebted to one another. Such is the heart of Sabbath celebration.

By liberating this poor woman crippled by a 'spirit of weakness', Jesus is enacting his manifesto pledge. He was initiating the Jubilaic Age ('the year of the LORD's favour'), the age of debt-amnesty, when all debts are written off and all debt-slaves are freed. What more fitting moment for the liberation of a woman who was the embodiment of poverty, to find liberation than on the Sabbath day?

The synagogue leader was clearly oblivious to the historic drama unfolding under his very nose. In his bowels, he felt neither the plight of this woman, nor the essence of the Jewish Law. The tragic irony of this story is that sabbath (from the Hebrew word meaning 'stop') – is supposed to be a practice in which Jewish worshippers withdraw from the busyness of daily life to take their coordinates in relation to their God and their world. Rabbi Abraham Joshua Heschel described sabbath as 'a palace in time', a moment of profound self-reflection and self-awareness – as every Israelite re-discovers their true place in the universe. By Jesus' day, it had become a law so encased in subsidiary regulations it was almost impossible for poor people to obey it. Failure to observe sabbath regulations would in turn render them, 'sinners', leaving those most in need of liberation only further alienated from God. This was what prompted Jesus to remind his hearers that originally, 'sabbath was made for people, and not people for the sabbath' (Mk 2:27).

Sadly, for my younger brother (to whose memory this book is dedicated), the debt-freedom that sabbath promises was never fully realised. He was one of the numberless folk whose actual plight rarely features in the deliberations of neoliberal policy-makers, the pontifications of hipster-moralists, the denunciations of the self-declared woke-ists, or the heartfelt (but bowel-less) prayers of the pious. Like the synagogue leader, they all too often remain oblivious to the historic drama unfolding under their very nose. But Jesus has nevertheless blasted his jubilaic horn (Lk 4:18-19).

FORGIVENESS

Forgiveness is often understood as a spiritual transaction, where I can wipe clean my moral slate because I have done something to make up for the wrongdoing I have committed. Forgiveness, however, above all else – means debt cancellation. And Jesus lived under an empire that demanded all citizens to honour their debts, not cancel them. Jesus' teaching on forgiveness is going to get him into serious trouble.

> *Then Peter came and said to Jesus, 'Lord, how often shall my brother sin against me and I forgive him? Up to seven times?' Jesus said to him, 'I do not say to you, up to seven times, but up to seventy times seven.'*
>
> *'For this reason, the kingdom of heaven may be compared to a king who wished to settle accounts with his slaves. When he had begun to settle them, one who owed him ten thousand talents was brought to him. But since he did not have the means to repay, his lord commanded him to be sold, along with his wife and children and all that he had, and repayment to be made.*
>
> *So the slave fell to the ground and prostrated himself before him, saying, "Have patience with me and I will repay you everything."*
>
> *And the lord of that slave felt compassion and released him and forgave him the debt.*
>
> *But that slave went out and found one of his fellow slaves who owed him a hundred denarii; and he seized him and began to choke him, saying, "Pay back what you owe."*
>
> *So his fellow slave fell to the ground and began to plead with him,*

saying, "Have patience with me and I will repay you."

But he was unwilling and went and threw him in prison until he should pay back what was owed.

So when his fellow slaves saw what had happened, they were deeply grieved and came and reported to their lord all that had happened. Then summoning him, his lord said to him, "You wicked slave, I forgave you all that debt because you pleaded with me. Should you not also have had mercy on your fellow slave, in the same way that I had mercy on you?" And his lord, moved with anger, handed him over to the torturers until he should repay all that was owed him. My heavenly Father will also do the same to you, if each of you does not forgive his brother from your heart.'

(Mt 18:21-35)

An old fictional story circulating in various forms, runs along the following lines. After a visit to the pub, two guys go to the theatre and settle down to watch the play. The show turns out to be terrible. One of the two friends is bored, but soon finds himself in desperate need to empty his loosened bowels, so disappears in search of the toilet while his friend watches his seat. The toilets were not well signposted. In his search, the increasingly desperate man wanders further into the recesses of the theatre until he finds an empty room with a large plant pot in the corner. Squatting above the pot, he releases the contents of his intestines and hurries out. When he returns to his seat, his friend says, 'You just missed the best part: some guy just ran across the stage and shat into that plant pot.' The point is not dissimilar to that made by Jesus in the parable cited above and today may serve as an indispensable complement to that parable. As usual, modern readers are unlikely to identify themselves with the villain of the story. Surely, if we had our own major debts cancelled, we would be perfectly happy to forgive the minor debts of others. The fact that we have understood the parable, allows us to look down with disdain upon the utter selfishness of the parable's hypocritical villain. But the parable is more sophisticated, and the situation more commonplace than many might imagine.

As the Lord's Prayer has shown, there is virtually no ethical difference between forgiving sins and forgiving debts. Here, sin and debt are virtually interchangeable. Sin, after all, originally meant debt. In Anglo Saxon England, for instance, if one person wronged another then, in order to prevent violence, a monetary fine was attached to the crime. The level of the fine was determined by the value of the offended man (was he a peasant, a yeoman, a woman, a lord or a king?), and the severity of the offence (a black eye or a severed limb?). Until the offended party had been paid off, the offender was in debt – a state of distress requiring a financial settlement. To forgive the sin was to forgive the debt and vice versa. The same relation between sin and debt finds its way into the Lord's Prayer as Saint Luke reports it:

Forgive us our sins,
Because we have already cancelled the debts *of all who owe us.*
(Lk 11:4)

The implication is simple. If you're asking God to forgive you for any wrongdoing, then you will have already cancelled all debts due to you by other individuals. Otherwise, you are the villain in the parable.

In Jesus' day, falling into debt usually had nothing to do with individual wrongdoing, but with the culpability of creditors who forced vulnerable individuals into debt. Did those creditors still worship God? If God himself has forgiven all the sin/debt of an individual, how can that individual remain in financial debt to a wealthy Israelite? If a Palestinian peasant is granted a 'clean slate' by Yahweh, how can any Israelite creditor fail to do likewise? Forgiveness – as Jesus teaches it – dictates that within faithful Israel, no-one can remain in debt to anyone else.

The implications for Jesus would prove disastrous. People opposed his teaching on forgiveness not because he taught that God forgives peoples private wrongdoing – but because he taught that God delegitimizes debt. Powerful but pious wealthy leaders could hardly tolerate that! When Jesus initiated an entirely new era characterised by forgiveness / debt-cancellation

(Lk 4:18-19), he threatened economic and political norms that favoured the powerful. As the economic historian Michael Hudson has claimed, Jesus was killed because of his economic policy.

How does this translate into the economic situation of the twenty first century? In the UK and the US for instance, the national debt (deficit) is nothing like the debts of a state or an empire. Today the chains of cause and effect are threaded through complex economic machinery that protects beneficiaries from confronting the human consequences of their comfort and prevents those who suffer from identifying the cause of their poverty. The ethical elements of economics are swept beneath a carpet of convoluted language and incomprehensible structures. This teaches today's unwitting creditors to enjoy their status without any hint of guilt, and debtors to accept that their status is just 'the way things are'. Everyone shrugs their shoulders and declares 'people have to pay their debts' (Though anyone who has genuinely celebrated Sabbath also will be asking 'why'?)

When a nation (with freedom to print its own currency) carries debt, it is nothing like household debt. In this light, tightening our belts to clear the debt (austerity) is – according to Modern Monetary Theory – woefully unnecessary and does little more than promote economic inequality. (It was precisely in order to remove such inequality that Jewish leaders had long since promoted the economic disciplines of Jubilee, Sabbath and forgiveness). This, in turn, means that wealthy members of a society who insist on imposing austerity on others are, in effect, running across the stage and shitting into a plant pot. After all, being the beneficiary of an economy that inflicts harsh measures on others is tantamount to experiencing forgiveness (lack of debt) but denying it to others (demanding that debts are paid by those weaker than ourselves). For someone to support austerity without being exposed to the harsh realities it brings for so many, is precisely the attitude of the villain in Jesus' parable.

THE PRODIGAL SON (Part 1)

The parable (as a form of rhetoric) is an ideological explosive device, a literary mechanism designed to jolt hearers out of one worldview to land them in another. Jesus has long since been locked in debate with Pharisees who were now outraged that he was identifying himself with 'sinners'. Jesus uses this story both as a defence against the charge of mixing with the wrong people, and to launch an offensive against those who fail to embrace the 'shit of the earth.'

> *Jesus said, 'There was a man who had two sons. The younger one said to his father, "Father, give me my share of the estate." So he divided his property between them. Soon after, the younger son gathered all he had, set off for a distant country and there wasted his wealth in a reckless binge.*
>
> *After he had spent everything, there was a severe famine in that whole region, and he found himself in need. So he went to work for a citizen of that country, who sent him to feed pigs in his fields. He wanted to fill his guts with the pods that the pigs were eating, but no one gave him anything.*
>
> *'When he came to his senses, he said, "How many of my father's employees have food to spare, and here I am starving to death! I will rise again, return to my father and say to him: Father, I have sinned against heaven and against you. I am no longer worthy to be called your son. Make me like one of your employees." So, having risen up, he went to his father.*

'However, while he was still in the distance, his father saw him and his bowels were churning; he ran to his son, threw his arms around him and kissed him...
(Luke 15: 11-20)

This parable is generally known as *The Prodigal Son,* prodigal meaning excessive/lavish/ wasteful. It is, at every level, a story about human waste. The father in the story is no less wasteful than his wayward son, lavishing all manner of undeserved gifts on his unworthy offspring. Such wasteful behaviour did not sit well with the economic measures of love permitted by a culture obsessed with honour and shame.

Regardless of its merits, the ideology of honour and shame quietly produces human beings trained to be outraged by trivia and to trivialise the outrageous. The first part of the parable focuses on making a mountain (of shame) out of a molehill (of failure). The reason is straightforward. The honour/shame culture is designed to enable a social hierarchy to run smoothly. Those with honour (be it earned, or inherited) may rise to the top. Those without honour (having been born without it or squandered it) belong at the bottom. Ultimately, this enables the economy to serve the over-privileged (without a trace of ethical protest), society to police itself, lower class outrage to be directed sideways (to peers) but not upwards (to superiors), and elites to maintain control of the masses.

The contemporary ideology of neoliberal capitalism is no less toxic and no more visible to us than ideologies of honour and shame were to those of our ancestors bound within them. We are still programmed to accept the upward transfer of wealth (never bothering to investigate or protest how and why this happens) and to demonise those who threaten this status quo (whistle blowers who reveal war crimes, politicians who aren't for sale, journalists who still speak truth to power). We are still programmed to direct our anger at one another (identity politics) rather than at those who create misery (moneyed interests, the politicians they have bought and the media channels they own). We are still programmed to be outraged by trivia (celebrity scandals, politically incorrect tweets etc) and to trivialise the outrageous (the use of war to expand wealth, the economic laws draining hope itself from those who possess little else, and the ecological terror that threatens the future of our species). If there is such thing as a human future, our generation – including its Christian celebrities, its cultural pundits, its unwittingly closed-minded academics, its free-thinking socially-minded liberals – will one day be viewed as no less deluded, no less complicit in injustice, no less indifferent to the suffering we create, no less self-righteous than those pitiable folk trapped inside ancient cultures of honour and shame. If anything, the sneering delusional conviction that we are above all that reveals how we are more pitifully submerged beneath it than ever our ancestors were.

It is precisely Jesus' ability to exorcise this toxic cultural spirit that revealed his status as a prophet. This explosive parable achieves just that.

In an ancient Mediterranean society obsessed with honour and shame, for a father to consent to dividing his property amongst his offspring – though permissible by law – was unacceptable to cultural convention. The younger of two sons would be entitled to one third of the father's estate, and this portion would then be sold off – diminishing the size of the family property, exposing the community where they lived to outside investors and jeopardizing the social integrity of the village. More importantly, for a son to request his inheritance whilst his father is still alive, is not only to wish his father was dead, but to demonstrate the father's failure to command the respect of his children. A family's share in the land was crucial to the wellbeing and reputation not only of the family, but of the entire community. For the son to have parted on these terms, was to subject the villagers to risk and shame and to expose the father to their scorn and ridicule. Consenting to the son's departure is already the action of a failed father.

The outrage mounts, however, when a wayward son dares to show his face in the village and returns to the family he had disavowed. It is the ultimate walk of shame, a failed act of rebellion, a wasted fortune, all of it carried back into the village on the shoulders of the son who returned with his tail between his legs. What would be the correct response to such a homecoming? The correct moral reaction of the villagers would be to kick the shit out of him and send him on his way long before he got anywhere near his family. Why did this not happen in the parable? Because, 'while he was still in the distance… His. Father. Saw. Him.'

Who did the father see from a distance: a failure, a rebel, an idiot, a threat, a disgrace? Quite probably all of these at once, but after months and possibly years of absence, he saw – above all – his son. The father's reaction was irrational, undignified, and utterly defiant of social convention – because it was the father's bowels that drove him to action. It was quite literally a 'gut reaction'. He girded his loins (i.e., pulled his pants up) and went haring through the village to welcome and protect his son. In other words, it was his bowels that empowered him to tare through the cast-iron barriers of righteous alienation as though they were budget bog roll.

The power of bowel eruptions to expose the stupidity of a dehumanising economic ideology has been wonderfully demonstrated in an hilarious, crude, low-tech but brilliantly edited 1980s satire entitled, *The Farting Preacher*. The preacher in question is the televangelist, Robert Tilton. He is infamous for teaching that poverty is sin, exhorting gullible viewers to show their faith by sending $1000 'vows' to his ministry, pushing an ideology that drains money from already-empty pockets, to line his own already-overflowing pockets.

The satire selects video clips from the preacher's appeals and mercilessly exploits his over-acted facial expressions. It then injects an impressive array of crude fart noises into Tilton's embarrassingly dramatic pauses: the ass-rattle of a steamy crevice-burst fills the gap that precedes, 'God is opening the windows of heaven'; a reverberating pile-driver echoes before words uttered in astonishment - 'I've had three or four of those in the last month'; and the claim 'I can feel God's cooking something up for you,' is followed momentarily by a thunderous rectal-snort of soggy warmth and a sickly grin. Having studied the clip several times, I was both surprised and disturbed at how gut-wrenchingly amusing I found something so crude. Beelzebub himself, it seemed, was somehow blowing his nose through Tilton's cack-flaps. I almost laughed myself into an alternative reality. Such is the potency generated by human bowels.

It is tempting of course, to denounce Tilton as a godless rectum-headed blowhard – but I am then in danger of being outraged by trivia. Before stoning him to death on Twitter, it is worth pausing to ask whether my missiles might boomerang on me. Am I really so different to the farting preacher and his victims? Do I merely prefer those who exploit the poor to do so with more tact, more taste, more style and a more subtle economic ideology? Is the greed of the televangelist simply one intolerable symptom of a wider economic injustice I would passionately defend? And then I wonder whether the protective father of the story might need to run from his house in order to defend his son against me? Might I be the reason for a movement in the father's bowels?

To ask yourself that question is to understand the parable.

THE PRODIGAL SON (Part 2)

Since Jesus' godly opponents have attacked him for socialising with (and thereby, endorsing the behaviour of) sinners, he has lobbed a rhetorical grenade into their holy midst. The first part of the parable demonstrates how these pious folk – like most others – have been programmed to make a mountain (of shame) out of a molehill (of moral failure). In the second part, he will now demonstrate how they equally make a molehill (failing to recognise a near miracle) out of a mountain (the gargantuan feat of restoring a broken relationship).

'The son said to him, "Father, I have sinned against heaven and against you. I am no longer worthy to be called your son..."

But the father said to his servants, "Quickly! Bring the best robe and put it on him. Put a ring on his finger and sandals on his feet. Bring the fattened calf and kill it. Let's have a feast and celebrate. For this son of mine was dead and is alive again; he was lost and is found." So they began to celebrate.

'Meanwhile, the older son was out in the field. When he approached the house, he heard music and dancing. So he summoned one of the servants and asked what was going on. "Your brother has arrived," he said, "and your father has killed the fattened calf because he has him back safe and sound." The older brother grew angry and refused to go in. So his father went out and pleaded with him. But he answered his father, "Look. All these years I've been working for you and never disobeyed your orders. Still, you never gave me even a young goat so

I could celebrate with my friends. But when this son of yours who has devoured your legacy with prostitutes comes home, you kill the fattened calf for him!"'

"'My son," the father said, "you are always with me, and all I have is yours. But we had to celebrate and be happy, because this brother of yours was dead and is alive again; he was lost and is found."'

(Luke 15:21-32)

The son's return to the home he had so drastically damaged would have been a terrifying prospect, and an experience that warrants further reflection. He does not merely face a little social awkwardness. The terror he felt as he approached the village would have run far deeper than the fear you might feel when facing down a game of Twister after a feast of beans. In accordance with cultural conventions that he had no reason to challenge, the villagers would do far worse than sneer at him, his family would be unable to conceal their fury at him, and it was by no means guaranteed his father would even employ him. But driven by desperation, he accepted his status as an outcast, forfeited his rights as a son, acknowledged that he wreaked of shame and sought nothing more than minimum wage.

As he enters the village his father comes impulsively hurtling across the fields so fast, he left his dignity behind. Crashing into an unexpected embrace the son begins to rehearse the confession he had prepared, but his father is so overcome with emotion he interrupts. As his servants arrive on the scene, he issues orders to lavish on his son all the gifts associated with success in an honour/shame society of rewards and punishments. Before long an extravagant party is underway, designed for the dual purpose of appeasing the otherwise disapproving villagers and publicly bestowing honour on a son who had squandered all honour of his own. Like everyone present at the dinner, the son would have expected (because he deserved) to sit in shame and eat cauldrons of his own shit. Now he is seated in a place of honour, eating the fattened calf. But there is a terrible absence.

The older son is not happy. He had brought no shame on the family. And yet the father had lavished no gifts and no honour upon him. According to the moral measures of an honour/shame society, the older brother is justified. His anger is righteous. In Hebrew thought, anger arises from the nostrils – it flares up, just as juices might swell inside a plant. Compassion, as we know, arises from far deeper inside the human spirit – in this instance from within the bowels of the father.

Before distancing ourselves from the angry judgmentalism inherent within an honour/shame culture, it is worth pausing again to consider just how different our world isn't. If today's multi-billion-dollar PR industry is not a gigantic waste of money – it will be training you and me to swell with anger at the prescribed issues, whilst keeping us safe in the delusion that we ourselves (as intelligent, educated, insightful and moral beings) are beyond its reach. It will have quietly reduced us to an infantile dependence on 'mainstream media' (itself a phrase hated by those old-school influencers whose livelihoods are comfortably afloat on its toxic stream). That is, a media machine that spoon feeds us the contents of our own potty whilst assuring us we have a healthy intake of information. The notion of 'information' is telling in itself. To be informed is, strictly speaking, to undergo an 'inner formation' of belief, attitude, outlook and behaviour. We may well be no more healthily well-in-formed than the older brother in this story.

Formed in what way? As Charlie Brooker notes, 'Newspapers chiefly exist to spoon-feed the opinions of their readers back to them, much like an arse-to-mouth hosepipe.' And just to be clear, 'newspapers' here includes the formerly liberal and historically progressive daily creeds of the righteous intelligentsia, as well as the soft-porn right-wing hate-instructions issued to the semi-literate masses. Universally, we are fed a similar diet to that of the older brother in the story. Just as the older brother slipped the unfounded allegation of prostitution into his brother's list of crimes, so we are trained to imagine our enemies committing terrible crimes of which they may be innocent: Whistle-blowers, Occupy, Extinction Rebellion, Socialists, Trumpists, Clintonites, Blairites, Corbynites, Brexiteers, not to mention whoever our imperial guns are pointing towards this year: Russia, Syria, Iran, China, Wales... And if they are innocent of our poorly grounded accusation, does it really matter? They are terrible after all, so probably deserve a good shit-flinging. A well-functioning media machine can magically transform molehills of shaky evidence into mountainous crimes obvious to any sensible intelligent person. Those nasty, ignorant, deluded people out there who are nothing like me, thus deserve to be ridiculed, humiliated, defeated, ashamed, and possibly destroyed, all for the sake of righteousness. But maybe the reason we expect our enemies to eat cauldrons of their own shit, is that this has long been our own time-honoured staple diet.

The healthy bowels of the father, however, drive him to kick the mountain right down. It was only a molehill after all (see Matthew 17:20). By counteracting the culture of hostility with bowel-driven acts of kindness, compassion and love, he has trivialised that which should always have been trivial – the obvious moral failings of his own child. The basis of the father's appeal to the older brother is to recognise the real mountain that actually looms before them. 'This your brother' (the older brother had disowned the younger), 'was dead and is alive again. He was lost and is found.' At the heart of Israelite identity were the relational bonds that ran within and between families – bonds of togetherness that ran through the long centuries all the way back to Sarah and Abraham, and bonds that ran so inexplicably deep they channelled an otherness that the Jewish people called, 'Yahweh'. The severance of that bond is an utter tragedy. The younger son had been truly lost. To repair that severed bond is to restore life where there had been alienation, longing, and death. This successful ethical surgery was a beautiful and outrageous restoration for the entire family – all of which the older brother has trivialised. The older brother has forgotten, in other words, what it really meant to *be* Israel. He is in danger of becoming lost himself.

THE FATE OF PROPHETS

As Jerusalem begins to loom larger on Jesus' horizon, some well-meaning Pharisees arrive, warning him to keep moving now that he is on the radar of the Galilean ruler. Herod's plan is to silence the prophetic agitator, and to disband the crowds that follow him. But Jesus shifts his focus to Jerusalem, the Holy City whose gravity is drawing him ever closer. Jesus is well aware of the fate that awaits him there. As a prophet, he will 'speak truth to power', and in reply, that 'power' will come down on him in all its vicious brutality.

At that very time some of the Pharisees came and said to him, 'You should leave and go from here, because Herod intends to kill you.

And he said to them, 'Go and tell that fox, 'Look: I drag demons out and perform healings today and tomorrow, and on the third day I will be finished. It is inevitable that I must be underway today and tomorrow and the day after tomorrow, because it is impossible that a prophet is killed outside Jerusalem'.

'Oh, Jerusalem! Jerusalem! Who kills the prophets and stones those sent to her. How often I have intended to gather your children, just as a hen gathers her brood under her wings. But you would not have it. And now look: your house is abandoned to you. But I tell you, 'you will not see me until such time as you come and say, "Blessed is he who comes as the Lord's representative."'

(Luke 13: 31-35)

As a young nervous military recruit, I had been armed with a 7.62mm self-loading rifle and ordered to occupy a pillbox (a concrete defensive bunker) with two other steely-eyed killers. On a cold December morning, we were boldly defending the unsuspecting Lincolnshire country folk from imminent attack either from Russian special forces or non-existent terrorists. At any moment we could have been bombed, shot, gassed, nuked or ridiculed, and so we remained hyper-vigilant. After only a few minutes, a loud bang thundered from the nearby treeline, followed by the squawk of birds as they fled. And then... silence. A look of sheer terror spread across my comrade's face as he looked at me. In an instant, my nostrils filled with a reeking menace. Overpowering in intensity, it scorched my nasal hairs and wrought deadly mayhem as it entered my lungs. This was it. Hoping I was not too late, I reached for my respirator, secured it properly, blew out hard and shouted 'Gas! Gas! Gas!' – all in accordance with our training. The three of us came piling out of the gas-filled bunker and took up defensive positions amidst the bushes outside.

Our combat instructor came striding through the trees, bellowing at us to stand up and remove our respirators. 'What the f**k are you doing?'

'We detected gas, corporal,' I answered.

He entered the pillbox and within seconds re-emerged, his sleeve covering his face. 'Okay, who's shit themselves?'

My terror-stricken comrade raised his hand. The corporal smacked him around the head and sent him to change his underwear – rebuking him as he went for inadvertently launching a chemical assault through his unmanageable crack-sphincter. Then he smacked me on the shoulder and almost reluctantly growled, 'Good shout.'

The bio-chemical atrocity my comrade had unleashed illustrates vividly the role of the prophet. Most people today regard prophecies as predictions of forthcoming events, and prophets as seers who foretell the future. But above all, a prophet is someone who farts into an enclosed space, forcing everyone to scramble over one another to escape. This is certainly how the prophets in Israel functioned, although the 'enclosed space' is – of course – metaphorical. The prophet can transform the security of a comfortable environment into an uninhabitable chamber of hostility – just like that toxic-fumed pillbox.

Today's metaphorical pillbox is called the 'Overton Window'. Once a useful tool, it has been overused and ridiculed, co-opted by those whose cowardice and complicity it might once have revealed. Nevertheless, it remains serviceable as a descriptive lens of humanity's current predicament. On the wide spectrum of human beliefs and attitudes, the Overton Window refers to the limited range of opinion (within that wider spectrum) that is currently deemed acceptable by 'public opinion'. If you are too far to the left end of the wider spectrum, you are 'outside' the window, and will be labelled radical or even terrorist because you are socialist, Marxist, hopelessly utopian, naively idealist, etc. If you are too far to the right end of the wider spectrum, you are 'outside' the window again – but this time will be labelled radical or even terrorist because you believe in fascism, racism, xenophobia, homophobia etc. Anyone outside the window must be perceived as the victims of propaganda, fake news and ideology. Safely within the Overton Window, are the sensible people like me.

The Overton Window, however, is not static. Within the wider spectrum, the acceptable range of public opinion can shift towards the left (though usually only in terms of social issues like equality of gender, race, religion – never financial equality). It can also shift towards the right (though usually only in terms of economic policies such as de-regulation, privatisation, welfare cuts). And how does the Overton Window move left or right on any given issue? Or in other words, who moves it?

The conviction that an entity called 'the public' has the freedom to form its own opinion, fails to account for the existence of the multi-billion-dollar Public Relations industry. This is an industry that has long since existed to shape public opinion – a crucial weapon in the arsenal of obscenely wealthy corporations to overcome the inconvenience of democratic accountability. Hardly surprising that today it has a friendly face (socially tolerant values) and an iron fist (smashing economic safeguards designed to protect unpeople from profiteers). Those trapped inside the Overton Window are carefully protected from seeing the world outside. (The psychological principle of

'What You See Is All There Is'). Worse still, they are sheltered from detecting the deadly cultural fumes that render them docile, complicit conformists – while intoxicating them with the belief that they are active, woke, rational, free-thinking justice-loving sensible folk. They will not thank anyone who marches into the sheep-pen, tears off their wolf-costumes, and farts into their fantasy. Plato saw the effects of all this, twenty-five centuries ago with his famous illustration of the cave.

The closest thing to PR industry gurus in Jesus' day were the Pharisees. Although they had no direct political power of their own, they were widely recognised as having enormous influence with the people. It is probably for this reason Jesus invests so much energy engaging with them. But they posed him little serious direct threat. When he entered Jerusalem however, he faced far greater powers. Those powers had a tradition of executing prophets. Not that they wandered around Jerusalem declaring 'no prophets allowed here!' Jerusalem (like all other cities and cultures) honoured its prophets – but only once those prophets lay safely and silently in their tombs.

This is a dynamic of which Jesus was well aware. He once confronted a group of Lawyers:

> *You build the tombs of the prophets, but it was your fathers who killed them. You are witnesses. You give your approval to your fathers' deeds. For they killed them and you do the building! Indeed, for this reason, the Wisdom of God said, 'I will send prophets and lieutenants to them, and some of them they will kill and persecute.'*
>
> *(Luke 11:47-49)*

That same self-deluding ethical retreat into 'hindsight bias' is no less prevalent in our own day. Prophets are and have always been honoured only by future generations who are safely beyond the prophet's gaze. The Civil Rights movement in the US and the Suffragettes in the UK – if they had appeared today would be deemed radical extremists, probably even terrorists. Within the Overton Window, it is much easier to venerate prophets than to hear them.

This is hardly surprising. Should we genuinely hear a prophet they will undermine much that has become precious to us. The PR industry has quietly trained us over long decades to suspect, to reject, and to eject them. Who, after all, would relish having their own slavish compliance with the venomous orthodoxies of extreme centrism, revealed for what it is? Many are perfectly at home in the toxin-rich pillbox of the Overton Window. Prophets are terrifying, and if they are not, it is because our fingers are in our ears. Whatever else Jesus may have been, he was nothing less than a prophet.

THE FRAGRANCE OF JESUS

Judas Iscariot has become a personification of evil. After all, he betrayed the only sinless earthling ever to float through this horrible world. In reality Judas was committed (he was among the Twelve who had given up everything to follow Jesus), he wanted to see his people freed from tyranny (why else would he have followed a liberator like Jesus?), and he did his best to make it happen (ensuring that God's anointed liberator came face-to-face with the tyrant). After all, if Jesus really were God's Messiah – he would be victorious. If he were not, this only meant he was not the Messiah. Even now, having arrived at the outskirts of Jerusalem, with his plot already formed, Judas' leftist convictions were still making social events feel awkward. The following story narrates how he rebukes Mary during a highly emotional interaction with Jesus, leading Jesus to respond, 'Do you mind – we're having a moment.'

> *Six days before the Passover festival, Jesus... came to Bethany... So they prepared him a supper there... Mary then took a pound of very expensive perfume of pure nard, and anointed the feet of Jesus and wiped his feet with her hair. The house was filled with the fragrance of the perfume.*
>
> *But Judas Iscariot, one of his disciples, who was planning to hand him over, complained, 'Why was this perfume not sold for three hundred denarii and given to poor folk?' Now he said this, not because he was concerned about poor folk, but because he was a thief, and as he had the treasury, he used to take what was put into it.*
>
> *So Jesus said, 'Leave her alone, so that she may keep it for the day of*

my burial. After all, you always have the poor with you, but you do not always have me.'
(John 12:1-8)

Many will know Graham Kendrick as the writer of the famous song, 'Shine, Jesus, Shine.' That song was once introduced by an earnest and over-excited worship leader whose liturgical enthusiasm tumbled his tongue into a semi-spoonerism as he encouraged the congregation to 'mean it' when they sang:

...

Fill this land with the Father's glory
'Blaze, Spirit, blaze
Set our f–hearts on fire'

Such an event – sometimes known to occur during an endoscopy – can be fatal. (Fart-ignitions, I mean, not spoonerisms). A minute electrical spark can ignite the methanic vapours in the large intestine and force an intracolonic explosion. This is a good metaphor for the religious disaster that destroyed Jerusalem a generation after Jesus' death. The toxic atmosphere in the city would soon ignite a full-blown national rebellion by those in search of 'the Father's glory'. The final result was that flames would engulf the holy Temple and end forever the ancient religion of Mosaic Judaism. This was always destined to be the fate of the 'satanic' programme of messiahship offered to Jesus in the 'temptation story' (Luke 4:1-13).

In the reading above, Jesus is anointed not for the purpose of seeking unselfconsciously satanic glory. Rather, expecting to face his own death, he is smothered in a costly fragrance as a prophetic act: perfume of this sort was sometimes administered to the recently deceased as they entered their tomb. By anointing Jesus with this perfume (and - according to Lk 7:44 - with her own tears), she was preparing him for his grave.

In the mid 1980s and with this imagery in mind, Kendrick also wrote a worship song about the 'fragrance of Jesus' that became extremely popular in several Church traditions. The imagery arises not only from the incident recounted above, but is rooted in the notion of the incense offerings of Ancient Israel and the pleasing aromas rising from sacrifices offered to Israel's God. After Kendrick's song, however, a new phenomenon spread among the charismatic churches of western Christendom: people began claiming to have undergone the supernatural experience of having 'smelt the fragrance of Jesus'. I have no wish to question the reality of this phenomenon – especially as a personal experience – but it is worth asking what, historically, that fragrance might have been.

In the modern west, so accustomed to showers, deodorant, perfume, air-conditioning, etc – consider the effects of going into the office one morning, having had no wash, no shower, no deodorant, and wearing a shirt you had to retrieve from the dirty laundry basket. By coffee time, your colleagues may have reported your suspicious activities to the NSA. By lunch time you'll have odorized your way onto a CIA watchlist. And you'll probably take your afternoon tea break at an undisclosed location wearing a blindfold and an orange jumpsuit. Smelling like a tiny mammal is decomposing somewhere in the brown foliage of your flesh-crevice is simply not acceptable in the modern world. If, however, you could jump into a time machine and jump out in first century Judea, your un-historicized nasal senses will have been trained to find everyone aromatically repellent. Were you able to locate the son of Mary and Joseph, and get yourself within sniffing distance, you might well find yourself running for fresh air because you had 'smelt the fragrance of Jesus.' There was nothing remarkable about messianic bodily odours, since nothing is reported about them. There are occasions, nevertheless, where he is adorned with perfume – very much an action associated with those who were wealthy and privileged.

Jesus' anointing in Bethany is one such example. Nard perfume was an extremely expensive substance, costing 'three hundred denarii'. According to the Gospels, a denarius was roughly an average labourer's daily wage (Matthew 20:2, John 12:5). As a hard-core progressive leftie, Judas Iscariot found this action a pointless extravagant waste. To his socially minded nasal cavity, the 'fragrance of Jesus' smelt like economic injustice. Like all who treasure liberationist aspirations, Judas was far from perfect and – no doubt

– was over-exposed to accusations of self-centredness and hypocrisy. It may also be John's anger at Judas' later actions that led him to accuse the demonized betrayer of helping himself to the group's campaign funding. This is not to say that the accusations are unfounded, but rather to consider how Judas' image has been presented by those whose hopes were demolished by the fateful consequences of his decision to report Jesus' whereabouts to the authorities.

It is impossible to know Judas' motives, but the fact that – after Jesus' execution – Judas committed suicide suggests that he had no intention of seeing Jesus come to harm. It seems most likely he had tried to force Jesus' hand, railroading him away from peaceful protest towards a *coup d'état*. This would certainly be consistent with the hopes of great swathes of the populace, and the bellicose mood that could seize the atmosphere of the annual 'Passover Celebration' soon to take place. This feast was a reminder to all pilgrims in Jerusalem, that their nation was founded on a great act of divinely violent liberation from pagan overlords. In Jesus' day this volatile celebration took place right under the hairy nostrils of a new hostile pagan super-power. All the ingredients for an 'intracolonic explosion' were in place every year.

The fact that, on such an occasion, 'satan entered Judas' (Luke 22:3) suggests not 'demon possession' as though a helpless and zombified Judas had lost all agency and responsibility. Satanism here (as in the 'temptation story') stands rather for a pattern of messiahship that seeks to fight violence with violence, assuming Jesus himself would come to no harm because he was God's Messiah. At other points in the narrative, this conviction had gripped Mary the mother of Jesus, John the Baptist, Simon Peter, and a host of others including those who would – the very next day – line the streets to welcome Jesus into Jerusalem. Judas' love for his people, his commitment to Jesus, and his longing for liberation all converged onto a moment when he could take decisive action. Tragically, he decided to deliver (this is all that was meant by 'betray') Jesus into the hands of those willing to use violence.

Within a week of this perfuming event in Bethany, Jesus' sweet-smelling body would become a mutilated corpse. Judas was then – literally – gutted.

According to Luke, for thirty pieces of silver he, 'bought a field – and there he fell headlong, his body burst open, and all his bowels burst out' (Acts 1:18). Satan had entered Judas and triggered an intracolonic explosion.

INNER PEACE

Jesus, knowing that he is likely facing his end, enters into lengthy discourse with his closest followers. He is now very near to Jerusalem, pilgrims from all over the Mediterranean world are arriving for the Passover festival, and as the city swells with excitable crowds that will soon condemn him, Jesus promises 'peace' to his followers. Given the violence and agony he knows he is about to undergo, it is difficult to know precisely what he meant when he spoke of peace.

> *All this I have spoken while still with you. But the Advocate, the Holy Spirit, whom the Father will send in my name - he will teach you all things and remind you of everything I have said to you. Peace is what I leave with you; my peace is what I give you. I do not give to you as the world gives. Do not let your heart be troubled and do not be afraid.*
> *(John 14:25-27)*

Christians have a sordid habit of stealing decontextualised bible verses that contain uplifting fluff memes, adding them to a scenic or cute photographic background, printing them on a poster and hanging them in their restrooms. One of the finest examples I recall loomed above the toilet of a childhood friend – whose parents had found a gloss-paper reddened sunset reflecting onto a beautiful lake to turn the still waters into liquid gold. The calming scenery was laced with the words, 'Peace I leave with you. My peace I give you (John 14:26)'. Any male stood emptying his bladder into the porcelain toilet bowl whilst facing those words, might half-expect to look down into the golden-piss-filled pan and read the words, 'well, thank you very much'.

There are many kinds of peace. The infamous Roman Peace (the 'Pax Romana') was a pacification ensuring that resources would flow freely from unpersons to elites – a notion that might better be described as 'order'. In ancient Hebrew thought, peace was that state of affairs when society is working properly and healthily – a notion that might better be described in terms of 'right-ness'. It was this state of peace or 'shalom' that enabled social justice to flourish. When this Hebrew grasp of peace penetrates the human heart and bowels, it suggests not 'order' but a deep-seated state of personal, relational, societal health. Patterns of – gulp – 'wellbeing' that have saturated the market today are more closely aligned with Roman notion of order rather than Hebrew notions of shalom.

Two first century Roman generals (Vespasian and his son, Titus) who – in order to impose order – invaded Judea and destroyed Jerusalem, both went on to become emperors. After a year of imperial disorder in Rome, Vespasian needed to raise funds in order to restore the Pax Romana. The most ingenious tax he raised was on the processed contents of human bladders – which was very widely recycled for the purposes of cleaning, bleaching, and tanning leather. When Titus criticised his father for imposing such a ridiculous tax, Vespasian was said to have shoved a coin under his nose and asked him whether it smelt bad. When his son answered, 'No' the father replied, 'Yet it comes from urine.' This is the origin of the phrase, 'money does not stink' (*pecunia non olet*). The imperial authorities were literally, taking the piss. But they were not the first.

A failed attempt to impose piss-tax was first made by Vespasian's predecessor, the infamous Emperor Nero. Ruling from 54-68CE, Nero was widely regarded a neurotic, despotic, psychotic, carnalised blend of mental health disorders. Many suspected him of starting the Great Fire of Rome (64CE) in order to clear ground for his new building projects – although Nero himself laid blame for the disaster at the door of a young and radically subversive movement known as 'Christians'. According to Tacitus, as the hungry flames engulfed two thirds of the sun-baked city (whose fires roared for six days)

Nero himself soothed his soul by playing his violin or 'fiddle'. Hence the phrase, 'fiddling while Rome burns.'

Regardless of whether the Nero story is true, the tradition has come to represent the insanity of engaging in frivolous self-indulgence in the midst of a crisis that screams for your attention. It is this precise brand of insanity that today is carefully packaged and marketed by the mental health industry. Via commodified forms of 'mindfulness', off-the-shelf models of counselling, and myriad other programmes for wellbeing, those suffering the effects of globalized socio-political arson today are encouraged to retreat from a combusting social world into the safe space of individual self-reflection. The most articulate critic of this so-called 'revolution' is Ronald Purser, who laments what happened to mindfulness techniques once they were severed from the ethical framework of their Buddhist origins:

> What remains is a tool of self-discipline, disguised as self-help. Instead of setting practitioners free, it helps them adjust to the very conditions that caused their problems. A truly revolutionary movement would seek to overturn this dysfunctional system, but mindfulness only serves to reinforce its destructive logic... by failing to address collective suffering, and systemic change that might remove it, they rob mindfulness of its real revolutionary potential, reducing it to something banal that keeps people focussed on themselves... (Purser, *McMindfulness*, 2019)

As we enter what may be the final century of human life on our planet, it is hardly surprising that the ecological and economic doom we have created for our successors are manifesting themselves in a mental health pandemic. And whilst various forms of mindfulness and self-reflection are essential in addressing this crisis, they are all-too-easily commodified and turned into profiteering ventures. Are our economic puppet masters, their PR machines and their politicians railroading us into oblivion? In any sane world, a healthy response would be to face this unholy Trinity head on and demand change. Our leaders are training us instead to sooth our souls as

Nero soothed his: by self-reflection, withdrawal from the world of politics, abandoning our negative thoughts and ridding ourselves of righteous anger. In other words, we are learning to fiddle while Rome burns. And we are deluded enough to call this mindless retreat from reality, 'mindfulness.'

I am not saying that all forms of mindfulness, counselling, and wellbeing strategies are useless – far from it. Only that, like anything of value in a world that favours profit over people, they have been turned against those they were designed to help. Corporate mindfulness rackets now sink a tranquillizer into the psyche of people whose political anger might otherwise unsettle the status quo. As Purser continues,

> Mindfulness, like positive psychology and the broader happiness industry, has depoliticized and privatized stress. If we are unhappy about being unemployed, losing our health insurance, and seeing our children incur massive debt through college loans, it is our responsibility to learn to be more mindful... The so-called mindfulness revolution meekly accepts the dictates of the marketplace. (Purser, 2019)

Seeking 'inner peace' while your external world crumbles is the worst kind of societal mental disorder. This is precisely how profiteers, corporations and investors protect their interests and defend the Pax Romana: by pacifying you. How? By moving your attention from the actions of the grotesquely unjust profit-making death-machine that rules the world, and into your own soul. Do you feel bad that our species is microwaving itself out of existence? Then the fault is yours, and you should jettison such negative thoughts. Ignore what's happening out there in the real world (unless the real world is failing to offer mindfulness courses).

Take the welfare provision offered by the University of Cambridge. It should hardly come as a surprise that Goldman Sachs are helping fund the mindfulness courses offered to students and staff of the university. It is crucial, after all, to train future employees to cower beneath the inhuman forces crushing the humanity out of the human condition. Your role – as a modern, enlightened, open-minded citizen – is to conform to the world as it is, not to challenge it. Is your world burning? Here, take this violin!

Jesus was a prophet who lived in the last generation of his people's existence as a Temple-focussed nation. But he did not offer them 'inner peace'. As he prepares to enter Jerusalem, he knows that his message will most likely be rejected and he himself will be executed as a terrorist. But within that apparently hopeless strategy of throwing his life against the unstoppable death machine of his day – he nevertheless offers his followers peace. Not a tranquillizer, the Pax Romanic sedative. That is, the 'inner order' where your personality is twisted into the inhuman shape of the empire that crushes you. He offers 'shalom', a peace that can be experienced only alongside others who, in actively and collectively resisting the omnipotent and oppressive gods of their age, encounter something that transcends their own short lives. That unspeakable, unmarketable 'something' is what he offers.

By any biblical standard, the global investment banks and major corporations of our own day constitute immortal, omnipotent, dehumanising gods that demand to be worshipped by the masses. And by kindly offering us mindfulness courses and narcissistic mechanisms for coping with the suffering they continue to impose – those gods are merrily pissing down our throat. As they empty their benevolent bladders into us, we can hear them smile, 'My peace I give you, my peace I leave with you.'

Worse still – by drilling mindfulness philosophy into our psyches – they have trained us to respond, 'Well, thank you very much'.

V

The Lion's Den

Jesus enters Jerusalem at the most fitting time: the Feast of Passover. The city was crammed full of Jewish worshippers, celebrating how their nation was born when God himself intervened to destroy an unstoppable military regime: the Egyptians. Naturally, tensions ran high at this annual festival, requiring the Roman prefect to bring in extra troops to maintain security and prevent any outburst of revolutionary fervour.

THE TRIUMPHAL ENTRY

A brigade of professional soldiers has been called into Jerusalem to keep the peace. And keeping it would be hard work. Crowds of pilgrims have flocked to the capital to remember how God miraculously delivered them from their oppressors, and to pray that history repeats itself in the present. No wonder the oppressors are there in force. This year, however, a Messiah is marching into Jerusalem.

Many laid out their cloaks on the road, while others spread branches they had cut in the fields. In front and behind, those who followed shouted,

'Liberate us!'

'Blessed is he who comes in the name of the Lord!'

'Blessed is the coming kingdom of our ancestor David!'

'Liberate us now, in the highest heaven!'

...

On reaching Jerusalem, Jesus entered the temple courts and began driving out those who were buying and selling there. He overturned the tables of the money changers and the benches of those selling doves, and would not allow anyone to carry merchandise through the temple courts. And as he taught them, he said, 'Is it not written: "My house will be called a house of prayer for all nations"? But you have made it a base of operations for terrorists.'

(Mark 11:8-11, 15-17)

In the mid 1990s I worked for a scaffolding company involved in rebuilding the aforementioned oil refinery on the Pembrokeshire coastline. Different shifts worked around the clock in different gangs, all sharing the same portacabins. At the central hub of our makeshift headquarters, was a flat-roof prefabricated structure proudly boasting a kitchen with both fridge and microwave. Mike (one of our day-shift scaffolders), however, found himself constantly frustrated that the night shift would – in the small hours – take and eat food he had left in the fridge ready for his breakfast the following day. Firstly, Mike began leaving polite post-it notes on his lunch box. Then, in light of repeated non-compliance, the notes became less polite – still with no effect. Eventually he took more extreme measures. One afternoon, having excreted a hefty log of dense, dry faecal matter, Mike then finished his shift by scooping it into a plastic bowl, marching into our headquarters, placing it in the microwave, setting the oven on full power, pressing 'start' and hurrying home while the night shift workers were still arriving. Witnesses later reported that the microwave gradually softened the cylindrical mass of chunky meat-wallop into a rancid bowlful of Luciferian bum-slurry. I was not present to inhale the intolerable fumes of diarrhoetic malice that finally engulfed the entire headquarters complex. Nor was the culprit – who had wisely vacated the premises before the knee-jerk recriminations of the night-shift began.

When I arrived at the refinery the following morning, I noticed the microwave lying on its side in the skip with all other manner of trash. Mike had committed gastronomic sacrilege and the electrical oven had been rendered forever unusable. In this light, his angry exploit constituted a 'prophetic act' very similar to that which Jesus committed in the Temple.

As I claimed of John the Baptist, Jesus was a prophet and prophets often communicated using prophetic action such as cutting hair, smashing pots, wearing an ox's yoke, and baptising Israelites. Jesus marched angrily into the headquarters of the Jewish religion, interrupting the legitimate routine of sacrifice with an act of violence, and vacating the premises before the recriminations kicked off. Precisely what Jesus' act signified remains a matter of debate amongst biblical scholars.

The best place to begin is to try to imagine oneself into Jesus' sandals. Jesus' messianic campaign had reached its climax. He had been born into a nation whose heritage was centuries of enslavement, racial memories of national defeat and exile, and present-day occupation by a hostile pagan superpower. But his was also the nation whose identity centred around a God of liberation, who freed Israel from slavery in Egypt, led them to the 'Promised Land', who enabled them to return there even after 70 years of captivity in distant Babylon, and who orchestrated a successful rebellion against the almighty Greeks.

However, it was the Romans who now ruled over Israel, and it was with good reason their emperors boasted the title, 'Omnipotent'. What then, did it mean to worship a God of freedom in a time of inescapable and omnipotent Roman oppression? Different groups within Israel had different ideas. Jesus had favoured revolution without a call to arms. He had favoured 'grace' as the most effective long term means of undermining abusive structures. He had counselled love for oppressive enemies, over-compliance with unjust laws, gratuitous generosity to undeserving antagonists. His messianic vision had generated new political structures (the radical origins of what later became known as 'churches'). His economic demands had encouraged solidarity within communities that were disintegrating under the weight of divisive tax laws (the radical origins of what later became known as 'forgiveness'). His ethical challenges had enabled widespread reversal of the dehumanising ideology of Rome (the radical origins of what later became known as 'sermons'). And yet, despite having amassed an enormous following, by the time he came to confront the tyrants who controlled the holy city, his plea to the nation had been largely misunderstood and his support was shallow. Tragic beyond description, his long anticipated and fateful arrival in Jerusalem, was a cosmic anti-climax.

When, in 2003, the US military machine rumbled into the heart of Baghdad, the streets were lined with citizens who cheered as they welcomed the troops. The crowds waved their hands, they waved flags, and – like those who had welcomed Jesus – they waved palm branches. The impression we have from the Gospel accounts of Jesus' 'Triumphal Entry' is that the excited crowds expected something similar. The military overthrow of a cruel, dictatorial rule. The people cried out, shouting 'Hosannah' – which traditionally is understood by churchgoers as a pious way of shouting 'hello' at God on a Sunday morning. In Jesus' day, 'Hosannah' really meant, 'Liberate us, now!' That was the expectation awaiting Jesus in the city that was bloated with pilgrims for the Passover. Pilgrims who had travelled from all over the known world to celebrate how Israel's God had defeated the omnipotent might of Pharaoh. Many of them hoped history was about to repeat itself, and that Jesus would be the one to make it happen. Unfortunately, Jesus did not rumble into the city in his Hum V or gallop in astride his war horse but entered on his ass. This was absolutely not the picture of a warrior king who had come to overthrow the Romans. Met with such militaristic hope, Jesus chose instead to overthrow the desks in the public courts of the Temple.

The scene in the Temple was one of utter chaos. Squawking animals, shouting disciples, angry traders, crashing tables, flapping birds, scrambling cashiers, angry worshippers, exits barred, entrances blocked, and above all the clutter and the noise, the raised voice of the Galilean builder. He cites Isaiah's hopes for the Temple as a 'house of prayer for all nations', precisely the brand of internationalism that had ended in such disaster at the outset of his campaign, back in his hometown. But now, at the end of his career, he has no reason to exercise caution. He claims that the guardians of the Temple cult had turned it into a 'den of robbers', or more accurately, a focal point for the militaristic nationalism that had gripped the nation. The word for 'robber' translates better today into a form of terrorism. The terrorism that so many Jerusalemites hated and feared. Desperation and deprivation had led many disenfranchised Israelites to become bandits, resorting to violence and robbery in order to survive. Jesus took this despised image of the outcast bandit and applied it to the beating heart of Israel's identity as a people. From that moment, his execution was inevitable. It could not happen just yet. The Temple courts were a massive complex, swelling with crowds, and making a swift arrest impossible.

The prophetic action he had performed, however, left an indelible mark. The impact was sacrilege. In the capital city of the cosmos, at the crown of Mount Zion, the 'blessed one' who 'comes in the name of the lord' had delegitimized the Temple complex and its ideology. This was no reformist. This was the action of a revolutionary. The prophetic action was a short term pause of sacrificial routine. It drew attention to how violent nationalism would lead to the permanent cessation of Temple practices. Jesus' actions in the Temple had rendered it unfit for purpose, as unusable as Mike's poo-tainted microwave. Just as the microwave ended up in the skip, within a generation the ornate craftsmanship of the Temple would be reduced to a gigantic mound of dusty rubble. The fate of the Temple was sealed. So too, was that of Jesus.

THE APOCALYPSE

As he neared his end, the great 16th Century reformer, Martin Luther, is reported to have likened himself to a turd: 'I am like a ripe shit and the world is like a gigantic anus, and we are about to let go of each other' (Luther, *Table Talk*). Jesus is similarly conscious of his own impending demise and describes the world around him in similar terms. According to Matthew's Gospel, this is Jesus' final block of teaching, and he uses it to describe the end of 'life as we know it'. Unfortunately, this has been interpreted by Christian religion into a discourse about the end of the space-time continuum. In so doing, the Church's attention has been drawn away from the horrors of the present, towards some end-of-the-multiverse event that is all in God's hands.

> *Jesus left the Temple and as he walked away his disciples approached and drew his attention to the Temple's architecture. So he asked them, 'You can see all these [buildings] can't you? Honestly, I'm telling you, not one stone here will be left on another. All of them will be demolished...'*
>
> *'Therefore, when you see the abomination of desolation which was spoken of through Daniel the prophet, standing in the holy place (let the reader understand), then those who are in Judea must flee to the mountains. Whoever is on the housetop should not go down to get stuff out of his house. Whoever is in the field should not turn back to get his cloak. But if you're pregnant or nursing babies in those days, you're screwed! So pray that your escape will not be in the winter, or on a Sabbath. Because then there will be massive turmoil, like nothing since*

the beginning of the world until now, nor ever will be again. Immediately after the turmoil of those days the sun will be darkened, and the moon will not share its light, and the stars will fall from the sky, and the powers of the skies will be shaken...'

'Now, learn the parable from the fig tree: when its branch has already softened and produces its leaves, you know that summer is near: you too, then, when you see all these things, appreciate that he is near, right at the door. Honestly, I am telling you, this generation will not pass away until all these things happen...'

'But of that day and hour no one knows, not even the angels of heaven, nor the Son, but the Father alone. For the coming of the Son of Man will be just like the days of Noah. For as in those days before the flood they were eating and drinking, marrying and giving in marriage, until the day that Noah entered the ark, and they did not understand until the flood came and took them all away.

So will the coming of the Son of Man be.

(Mt 24:1-2, 16-30)

Scatology is the study (*logos*) of poo (*scatos*) and is conducted not only by those who use German toilets (see above) but by Elvis fans, historians of shit, and authors of children's books. The first note on the Wikipedia entry for 'scatology' reads, 'not to be confused with eschatology'. The theological term 'eschatology' is the study of 'the end' (*eschaton*), usually taken to mean the end-of-the-world. Sadly, several decades before the benefit of all Wikipedian advice, the burger-loving Elvis Presley had indeed conflated the two. Elvis' condition today might be described as an eating disorder, not least because he is said to have consumed 10-12000 calories a day, around five hundred percent of a healthy calorific intake. For the King, scatology and eschatology finally collapsed into one when he met his tragic end on the toilet, straining to force a herd of burgerised cattle out through his tail-end crevice. His ominous toilet experience is by no means unusual.

The male line of my own family history, for instance, is plagued by the dread of bowel cancer. That one day, an unsuspecting sheet of pristine toilet paper will use its absorbent properties to soak up blood as well as excrement. Of course, such an experience may simply reveal that you have crammed an oversized mahogany rolling pin through a fleshy exit that just couldn't cope with the strain, that you have been scratching your arse without clipping your fingernails, or indeed, that you have been using bog-roll from a 1970s school restroom. Nevertheless, the first thing to do after an anal-blood-letting terror is to utter one of the Jewish prayers cited earlier in this book. Then secondly, by all means necessary, to avoid self-diagnosis informed by an internet search. And thirdly, to contact a medic without delay. It may be nothing. It may be a sign that, if left unheeded, foretells your own inability to distinguish between scatology and eschatology.

Jesus' final discourse is widely deemed 'eschatology' because it deals with 'the end'. In this instance though, Jesus is clearly not talking about the end of the universe. The teaching was triggered by the disciples' awe at the Temple, one of the most magnificent structures in the ancient Mediterranean world. In Jesus' day, the Temple was undergoing a massive renovation that was only completed just in time to be destroyed by the Romans in 70CE. Even if these yokels from provincial Galilee had been to Jerusalem before – they might still be witnessing this stunning architecture for the first time. Throughout their lifetime, the Temple renovations were constantly underway. Jesus simply draws attention to its fate. He has wiped the arse of Jerusalem and seen blood.

Corruption amongst oligarchic elites, keen to curry favour with imperial overlords, has spilled over into growing economic despair for the peasant populace. That despair is already gathering momentum towards a fateful act of national rebellion against Rome. There is nothing supernatural about foreseeing the eventual outcome. Imperial legions will conquer Israel, leaving a terrified populace having to *'flee to the mountains'* (hardly sound advice if the fabric of the entire cosmos is collapsing – but perfectly sensible on seeing a distant army hell-bent on destruction). When the war machine breaches the walls of Jerusalem, it will desecrate (*'the abomination of desolation'*) the Temple (*'the holy place'*) and *'demolish'* its fine stonework. The *massive turmoil* created (triggering decades of severe recriminations against

Jewish folk around the empire), is naturally described in end-of-the-world language. There is no other way to describe the loss of the Temple, the beating heart of the nation, the focus of their entire existence. Hence, *'the sun will be darkened', 'the moon will not give light',* and *'the stars will fall from the sky'*. As John Barton has quipped, it's not as though 'the rest of the country will have sunny spells and scattered showers'. The language is a metaphorical description of the end of an era, the end of life as we know it. For a faithful and pious Jerusalemite, the end of the Temple seemed like the end of the entire cosmos.

The *parable of the fig tree* is designed to alert hearers to what they should be able to see for themselves. In essence, it is not dissimilar to the lesson of toilet-paper-and-blood. Cause and effect. The outcome that is inevitable if left unchecked. And time is running out. This cosmic catastrophe Jesus foretold did indeed take place before his own *generation* had passed. In 70CE to be precise.

End of the world language is more appropriate in the twenty-first than the first century. As Roger Hallam, co-founder of Extinction Rebellion (XR) points out, the predicament of our planet is much like that of receiving a cancer diagnosis.

> ... If you carry on as normal, you're definitely going to die. Or you can try and change, but you might still die. Those are the options for the human race now, if we are to believe the science... When you go and see a doctor, you don't blame the doctor. You don't call him a revolutionary, because the doctor is simply telling you what the science is. And the science is: we're going to have social collapse; or we're going to try and do something about it. (Roger Hallam, Interview with Chris Hedges, 2019)

Like many when first hearing a cancer diagnosis, our world is unable to process the enormity of what must lie ahead if we are not to microwave our species out of existence. To push Hallam's insight a little further, we might appeal to the stages (or today, 'elements') of grief identified by Elisabeth

Kübler-Ross, namely denial, anger, bargaining, depression and acceptance. The vast majority of our planet remains trapped in denial – and let's be clear, this does not mean being a climate-change denier.

Denial includes those responses limited to serious but peripheral concerns – recycling, plastic reduction, and purchasing brand new eco-friendly motor vehicles. It also includes any media outlet that devotes less than 95 percent of its print-space or airtime to addressing how humanity might limit the scope of forthcoming global catastrophe.

Anger, of course, is often directed towards those groups like XR or, more recently, Just Stop Oil – as Hallam points out – that are highlighting uncomfortable truth.

Bargaining can be heard by every individual or organisation investing *all* hope in some form of technological solution to climate change, anything that allows our beefish addiction to fossil-fuel consumption to remain unthreatened.

Depression is manifested in an entire generation undergoing a mental health pandemic arising ultimately from their stolen future. Rather than risk a generational uprising, we bear down on them still further by offering only superficial, apolitical forms of counselling and mindfulness that do not address the root causes of this catastrophe. We convince them instead, that their depression is a result of 'their' individual problem, not 'our' collective economic and ecological complacency.

Given the overwhelming gloom that engulfs us, is there any room for hope? Rather than seeking some shallow, world-denying, ego-centric optimism, genuine hope lies beyond the traumatic encounter with the world as it is. *Acceptance* then, is the disturbing, self-denying, hard-won, necessary gateway to hope. This has been the logic of Jesus of Nazareth from the very outset of his campaign.

All manner of social, intellectual, self-justifying psychological defence mechanisms against this truth crowd in on us today – and I am more than willing to embrace them. That way, I can continue eating, drinking, loving – just like in *the days of Noah,* right up to the moment the floods engulf me. Merrily bounding on through my life, in Presleyan excess, I am happily compliant with my society's slow-motion, self-administered bovine overdose. The toilet paper is now covered in blood, but who cares? Once I flush the problem goes away.

THE SHEEP AND THE GOATS

Jesus was a divisive figure and told a parable to that effect. To many he is a king, a liberator, a warrior who will liberate his people from oppression and kick the arse of a hostile empire. To those who have been paying attention, he has a different model of kingship.

'But when the Son of Man comes in his glory, and all the envoys with him, then he will sit on his glorious throne. All the nations will be gathered before him and he will distinguish them each from the other, as the shepherd separates the sheep from the goats. He will put the sheep on his right, and the goats on the left.

'Then the King will say to those on his right, "Come, you who are blessed of my father, inherit the kingdom prepared for you from the foundation of the world. Because I was hungry, and you gave me food; I was thirsty, and you gave me a drink; I was a stranger, and you welcomed me in; naked, and you clothed me; I was ill, and you visited me; I was in prison, and you came to me." Then people of justice will answer, "Lord, when did we see you hungry, and feed you, or thirsty, and give you drink? When did we see you a stranger, and welcome you in, or naked, and clothe you? When did we see you ill or in prison, and come to you?" The king will answer, "Honestly, I tell you, what you did for even the humblest of my kin, you did for me."'

'Then he will also say to those on his left, "Get lost, you hateful people, into the unending fire which has been prepared for the devil and his messengers; because I was hungry, and you gave me nothing to eat; I

was thirsty, and you gave me nothing to drink; I was a stranger, and you did not welcome me in; naked, and you did not clothe me; ill, and in prison, and you did not come to me." Then they will answer, 'Lord, when did we see you hungry, or thirsty, or a stranger, or naked, or ill, or in prison, and fail to care for you?" Then he will respond, "Honestly, I tell you, what you failed to do for even the humblest of my kin, you failed to do for me." These will go away into unending punishment, but the people of justice, into unending life.'

(Matthew 25:31-46)

I once worked at a church in central London that committed enormous resources to its work with homeless people. People in all manner of need entered through the doors seven days a week, and members of the church did their best to accommodate them. This can sound idyllic and perhaps romantically righteous, but I learned very quickly that there is nothing romantic about this work. It stank. It literally stank. My most treasured memory of the church was the work of a 'Church Secretary', a distinguished academic who had formerly held a very senior position in one of the city's top universities. Having walked into the foyer one Sunday morning, I witnessed him on his hands and knees, scrubbing at the carpet. One of our regular homeless visitors had arrived in a terrible state, walked through the front door of the church, and shat himself. I witnessed (and smelt) only the aftermath. But the image of a proud, retired, well-dressed and distinguished gentleman, on all fours scrubbing diarrhoea out of the carpet is forever etched into my memory. Regardless of the many concerns this incident had raised, the dignity of the alcoholic visitor with bowel difficulty, was paramount. Having arranged for our visitor to be welcomed, cleaned, re-clothed, fed and properly listened to, the distinguished gentleman abandoned his own dignity for the sake of our visitor's dignity, sank to his knees, and for 20 minutes used his highly skilled hands to clean human excrement out of the floor.

This was a perfect example of how incarnation might work: a man in his 70s, who epitomized upper middle-class white male privilege, and traditional

British stiff-upper-lipness-on-steroids, stooped on his knees scrubbing toxic stench out of the carpet with no conscious thought beyond the wellbeing of a homeless visitor. In that moment, he had become an incarnation of the self-giving loving-kindness (in Hebrew, *hesed*) of God himself. He had no recollection of the event until, three years later, I confessed how much of an impact it had upon me. Like the 'sheep' of the parable, he had to be both alerted to, and reminded of, his own ethical action.

This is almost the exact opposite of modern moral deliberations. When it comes to behaviour, it is often tempting to ask – in line with the great philosopher, Immanuel Kant – 'what am I supposed to do?' That is, our moral behaviour is a set of conscious actions that we choose to perform, using only our brilliant thinking minds. We can simply use our glorious brains to decide to do 'the right thing.' (Whether we are 'free' to do so is another question – often dislocated from the irrational distraction of the human body). Whilst consciously asking ourselves about 'the right thing' is occasionally a legitimate kind of question when confronted with specific situations, it is the tip of the ethical iceberg. The massive bulk of our ethical deliberation is more likely drifting around deep beneath the surface of our conscious thought.

How then, are we to come to terms with the unacknowledged ethical reality of who we really are as people? What kinds of questions might we be asking ourselves? An alternative and non-modern basis for ethics is to ask not 'what ought I to do' but rather, 'how have I been situated to experience the real?' (James Bernauer, in *Michel Foucault, Philosopher*, 1992, 46). This question, attributed to the French philosopher, Michele Foucault, addresses the context that has randomly shaped my entire ethos (my ideological assumptions, my family, my friendships and my self-understanding, my belief and my action, my history and my future). How has all this random, overpowering influence over my positioning in this little corner of history, how has it all predetermined even the way I reflect on my place in the world?

The temptation for academics is to apply this kind of question solely to philosophical reflection, to pondering the lofty questions about ethics, or truth or nature or God, in sum – what A-Level Religious Studies students call, 'ultimate reality'. But for Foucault, it is also the kind of question any real academic will be asking whenever they swipe their credit card, whenever they book a flight, whenever they watch a news report, when they affirm or lament the opinions of others, when they enter a voting booth, when they boil their water, cook their meal, wash their face, wipe their arse, flush their toilet. It is from within these most mundane, social, bodily experiences that our true position in relation to the world is most fully revealed.

It is much easier to limit the scope of our ethical self-reflection. Take 'political correctness'. Without ever having to be exposed to the shit-filled realities of the other, you can just learn to couch misogyny, bigotry, and racism beneath an acceptable veneer of peer-approved language. Without ever lifting a finger to do anything about the plight of persecuted minorities – all you need 'do' is sneer at people who haven't learned or won't use your deodorised discourse. Behold, hypocrisy: moral rules 'up there' somewhere, that don't interfere with who I really am 'in here' as a bodily creature.

Conversely, portacabins are full of foul-mouthed unpersons who are disgracefully and disgustingly politically incorrect: Brexit-voting, Trump-supporting, climate-change-denying racists. And yet I know today many who – despite being all these things – work in food banks, have given up their own security to fight on behalf of asylum seekers, and commit themselves at great personal cost to supporting the very people that the vast majority of liberal PC moral crusaders will never dirty their hands with. Regardless of how we might enjoy spouting moral truths on *their* behalf, throwing loose-change at *their* plight, or voting for parties that once-upon-a-time defended *their* interests, we don't ever dare dirty our paws with *them*. Unless we are located, in some significant way, alongside those we claim to support – what we 'do' on their behalf is more likely for our sake than theirs. We do nothing *for* them unless we are also *with* them.

And so, we return to the Foucaultian question: 'how have I been situated to experience the real?' Is it a question that is only askable from 'outside' a situation where you might experience something real? Very few people scrubbing shit out of a carpet are likely to ask themselves this kind of question – because 'the real' has long since invaded their mind, their nostrils, their clothes, their skin, their bones, their routine, their reputation, their image, their psyche. By no means does this invalidate the question. But it might refresh such lofty reflection with a biblical backdraft.

There are plenty of thoughtful intellectuals who, on withdrawing from the nasty world to the safety of their study to ponder 'ultimate reality', might echo Jimi Hendrix: '... 'scuse me, while I kiss the sky'. Then there are plenty of pious folk, who might introduce God into their prayerful deliberations, and echo Bono: '...if you wanna kiss the sky, better learn how to kneel.' The lesson from my former church secretary takes this a stage further. 'If you wanna kiss the sky, better learn how to kneel in shit.'

THE GARDEN OF GETHSEMANE

It is near impossible to shake the image of a Jesus who, because he was God's son, had all manner of supernatural resources at his disposal to protect him from real life. It is easy to picture him with a Hollywood soundtrack, cool and dignified as he faces danger, defiant and in control as he prepares to go up against the might of the evil establishment. But there was nothing cool, or glamorous, or dignified or supernatural in what was soon to take place. This is all because: Jesus. Was. Human. Perhaps the best way to access the social and emotional dynamic here, is to imagine a person you might know and love, finding themselves in a lonely, fearful situation of mortal danger.

> *Jesus... went as usual to the Mount of Olives, and the disciples followed Him. When he arrived, he said to them, 'Pray that you don't have to undergo a trial.' And he withdrew from them about a stone's throw, knelt down, and began to pray, 'Father, if you are willing, remove this cup from me; yet not my will, but yours be done.' Now an angel from heaven appeared to him, supporting him. And since he was in agony, he was praying very intensely. His sweat became like drops of blood, dripping on the ground. When he got up from prayer, he came to the disciples and found them sleeping from anguish, and said to them, 'Why are you sleeping? Get up and pray that you don't have to undergo a trial.'*
>
> *... Now the men who were holding Jesus in custody were insulting him and hitting him. They blindfolded him and were asking, 'Prophesy,*

who is it that hit you?' And they were telling him all kind of things, blasphеming.
(Luke 22:39-46, 63-65)

In 1991, with two accomplices I sneaked out of a military base in Credenhill where I was in training, to access a cash machine in Hereford. Whilst there, we took the opportunity for a cheeky visit to a fast-food restaurant. I went in for a fillet-o-fish and came out with a broken nose. Having intervened in a civilian incident where physical abuse was being inflicted on innocent bystanders by an earthling of gigantic physical stature, I had stupidly assumed my superior physical prowess, simply on account of my being 'military'.

The delusion evaporated in a split second with a split lip, not to mention the arrival of his gang of bloodthirsty townsfolk. The evening then shifted rapidly from a fast-food restaurant, to a pursuit through the city, to the passenger seat of a police car that had just crashed, to a police station, and finally to a hospital – all in very quick succession. The beating I endured had not only broken my nose but left me with a bleeding lip and a black eye. The beating I administered had similarly resulted in a broken nose and the smashing of two teeth. Being hopelessly outnumbered (and in reality, outmatched) I fled through the streets – only to confront my colossal assailant again in Hereford Crown Court, several months later. I was parked unceremoniously in a court waiting room, accompanied only by members of the gang who had chased me through the city.

Now they glared at me and exchanged stories of what they had done to other victims stupid enough to resist them. When finally, the judge awarded me the sum of £200 for acting in the public interest, he peered over his glasses towards me and added, '...although next time Mr Perry acts in the public interest, he would be well-advised do so less violently.' Since then, despite being a boxer, I have feared physical violence far, far more than most.

Jesus of Nazareth was a young man. He was alone. And he was afraid. His fear manifested itself physically. Luke, an author often taken to be a medical doctor, notes that since Jesus was terrified by the prospect of all that lay ahead, his fear seeped out of his skin. Not only was he sweating. His sweat was *'like drops of blood'*, a rare condition known as hematohidrosis (literally, 'blood-sweat' in Greek). It is a reaction to acute fear. This condition has been recorded in soldiers before battle, sailors before a storm, victims before sexual abuse, and criminals before execution.

Jesus was no Socrates, bravely detached from his forthcoming demise. The aged philosopher in Athens calmly drank the deadly hemlock in accordance with the city's death sentence. Stoic in his resolve, he philosophised calmly with his friends as he prepared himself to slip quietly from life. In stark contrast, Jesus was facing beatings and torture. He was human, he was physically vulnerable, he was viscerally afraid, and he secreted blood.

He had already sealed his own fate by wreaking havoc in the Temple. But even as he knew the inevitability of being arrested, abused, clothed in an orange jump suit and executed, it is hardly surprising that he still entertained the notion of seeking a way out. He was arrested in a night raid, a slight scuffle ensued, and Jesus was taken to a 'black site' somewhere in Jerusalem. Then the beating began.

Whilst everyone experiences a physical beating differently, it is difficult for me to read these words without re-living the clunk and fuzz of being hit around the head, the metallic taste of my own blood slopping around my mouth, the numbness of blows that somehow don't hurt even as you can feel the damage they inflict. That same inability to process what is happening, numbing both sensation and fear. I always, though perhaps wrongly, assume that the 'agony' of anticipation Jesus felt in the Garden of Gethsemane has, by this stage, evaporated – despite the beating being a mere foretaste of the violence awaiting him.

Who would not be repulsed by the actions of these soldiers? They are nothing like me. I do not condone their actions, and it is difficult to imagine anyone would. The chief priests and elders of Jerusalem can be readily demonised for outsourcing their violence to their soldiers. But when I read of their role in Jesus' suffering, I find it hard not to recall countless conversations I have had with many a self-proclaimed pacifist. On learning of my violent history and interest in boxing, such pacifists – often with venomous aggression and smug moral superiority – are keen to tell me how, in contrast to me, they do not condone violence. As time passes, I become increasingly convinced that what they often mean is that they do not want to be confronted with their own violence, not least, the violence required to keep them in the comfortable life to which they have become accustomed. Now that I too am thoroughly pacifist (in theory if not in practice), to what extent do I condemn violence, only to expect others to commit it on my behalf? I find it hard not to believe that the vast majority of even the most enlightened, peace-loving, free-thinking, intellectual liberals actually support the actions of the soldiers they might unthinkingly condemn.

Take, for instance, our stance on whistle-blowers who are hounded mercilessly not only by governments whose crimes they expose, but by the media who once might have held those governments to account. Our role in this? Denouncing violence and war on the one hand, whilst remaining silent about the collective persecution of those who reveal the truth about our own war crimes on the other. It reveals our complicity with violence.

Remembering that 'belief' means, 'by life' – the way that we trudge through real life demonstrates that regardless of our high-sounding moral protestations to the contrary, we *believe* in violence. Yes, violence may repulse us – but that does not mean we don't support it. Like elders and chief priests, we outsource it, only to become angry when it boomerangs on us. The same is true of many people's reactions to Donald Trump. They are repulsed by him, longed to see him impeached, and hoped to bang him up in prison because he was a disgusting egocentric money-loving war-criminal. But what if Trump's role as a figurehead was – unwittingly – to hold up a mirror to the American people? What if he simply shows us who we really are, and what we actually believe? What if he is the hallmark of the very system with which we are happily compliant? An economic system that requires violence to be visited on people we don't ever have to encounter; a media system whose lies protect us from the truth about our collective selfhood; a political system that serves the market rather than the people. Trump is the logical, honest outcome of such systems. No wonder we angrily pretend Trump is just a bad apple, rather than a faithful and inevitable manifestation of our actual beliefs. No wonder we wanted a less disgusting successor. America's disgusting and violent values and practices could then be swept back under the carpet where they belong.

You and I are no more distant from the soldiers who beat Jesus than are the chief priests and elders who orchestrated his arrest. To pretend otherwise, is to descend further into complicity with their actions. In this light, I am causing the blood-sweat of Jesus. It is precisely people like me, of whom this young, lonely, courageous man was afraid. And I dare not deflect my outrage elsewhere. If I throw stones at these soldiers, I am likely to hit Jesus.

PONTIUS PILATE

Pontius Pilate was from the village of Fortingall in Perthshire. At least, according to an 1899 *New York Times* article. It simply goes to show how little we know for sure about Pilate. We cannot even be sure of his competence as a governor. He was certainly brutal, and appears to have been relieved of his post on account of that brutality. He also seems to have enjoyed antagonising his Jewish subjects. Beyond that we know little. Except, of course, that he returned to Perthshire to live out his post-prefect years. According to the *New York Times*.

> *Now Jesus stood before the prefect, and the prefect questioned him, saying, 'Are you the King of the Jews?' And Jesus said to him, 'so you say.' And as he was being accused by the chief priests and elders, he did not respond. So Pilate said, 'Do you hear how much evidence they bring against you?' But he did not answer him on any charge, and the prefect was astonished.*
>
> *Now it was the prefect's custom at the festival to release a prisoner willed by the crowd. At that time, they had a notorious prisoner whose name was Barabbas. So when the crowd had gathered, Pilate asked them, 'Who do you want me to release to you: Barabbas, or Jesus who is called the Messiah?' For he knew it was out of narcissistic self-interest that they had handed Jesus over to him.*
>
> *...*
>
> *The prefect said to [the crowds], 'Which of the two do you want me to release for you?' And they said, 'Barabbas.' Pilate said to them, 'Then*

> *what shall I do with Jesus who is called Christ?' They all said, 'Have him crucified!' And he said, 'Why, what evil has He done?' But they kept shouting all the more, saying, 'Have him crucified!'*
>
> *When Pilate saw that he was getting nowhere, but rather that a riot was brewing, he took water and washed his hands in front of the crowd, saying, 'I am innocent of this Man's blood; you can oversee that yourselves.' And all the people said, 'His blood be on us and on our descendants.' Then he released Barabbas for them; but after having Jesus scourged, he handed Him over to be crucified.*
>
> *(Mt 27:11-18, 21-26)*

A defendant accused of telling the truth about the war crimes of a powerful empire was wheeled into the court of a provincial vassal state. His only words were 'I plead not guilty'. Solely on the basis of those four words, the judge concluded that the accused individual was 'a narcissist who cannot get beyond his own self-interest.' Any further words from the defendant would thus have been futile, since the outcome of the case had clearly been decided in advance. It is probably for this reason Jesus opted to remain silent in the face of his accusers. He had the colossal weight of both the ideological and legal establishment bearing down on him. Jesus did not waste words, and this hearing was only going to end one way.

Pilate knew as much. His apparent reluctance to prosecute Jesus was more likely an expression of his long-standing hostility to the Jewish rulers of Jerusalem (Pilate was usually based in the coastal city of Caesarea), than of any desire for justice to prevail. Shedding the innocent blood of unpersons was a concern that simply did not register with anyone in Pilate's position. On another recent visit to Jerusalem, Pilate had massacred protesters by planting undercover soldiers amongst the crowd who – on his signal – clubbed many of them to death (Jos. Wars 2.9.4; Ant. 18.3.2). With this incident already carved into their collective memory, the crowds gathered before Pilate to bay for Jesus' blood were particularly courageous. Why, after lining the streets to welcome their messianic liberator, would they turn so quickly on him and demand his execution?

That the Jerusalem elites wanted to rid themselves of this prophetic agitator was understandable, but the people Jesus had come to liberate? Why did they turn on him? Because he was supposed to liberate them from Roman oppression, not Jewish corruption. He was supposed to level his wrath at the Roman garrison, not the Temple. This was neither the messiah nor the liberation they wanted. Barabbas, however, was a failed revolutionary. Although his attempt at violent insurrection had not succeeded, he did represent many of the hopes treasured by the gathered Passover crowds. With that in mind, can you imagine the courage required of those crowds? The courage to demand of a violent and powerful commander, that he release to the crowds a man who had attempted to challenge that violent commander? What was to stop Pilate butchering them? The cry for Barabbas to be released was a heroic, almost suicidal act.

Exasperated by the crowds' apparent contempt even for their own lives (something Pilate had witnessed before), the prefect engaged in a prophetic action. In full sight of the multitude, he famously *washed his hands* – presumably singing twice through 'happy birthday' to ensure he did a thorough job. But were his hands really clean?

When Sir James Dyson decided to bolt a Saturn V rocket to the wall of every restroom in the cosmos (including those of the Star Ship Enterprise), his intent was probably not to shower the multiverse with microscopic flakes of shit. But in his drive to flood the toilet market with his 'air-blade' hand-dryers, he had to dispose of the paper towel industry. And so began the privately-funded 'scientific' debate over which skin-drying method was better. In the course of the research that ensued, several studies found that – since most hands are not properly washed before being inserted into the high-tech machinery – what Dyson had invented was, in fact, a turbo-charged excretal distribution device.

For Pilate, washing his hands in an attempt to declare himself 'innocent of this man's blood' did not absolve him of his responsibilities of governance. His hands were still dirty. But translating his 'prophetic act' into 21st century political responsibility, lands us uncomfortably in the morality-meme, 'Not In My Name.' The sentiment behind this phrase is worthy and clear. Those who wave banners that bear the meme are seeking to distance themselves from the despicable actions of others. On many occasions, this can be a dangerous and courageous prophetic action.

However, precisely because the 'Not In My Name' phrase has proven so successful, it is then also taken up in the artificial dissent of the boutique activist. That is, the activists who believe themselves the righteous champions of justice, but whose activism aligns fundamentally and unwittingly with the interests of the greatest perpetrators of injustice: to be a mental health campaigner, whose only demand is for counselling provision that does nothing to address the root causes of mental health pandemic, in dutiful compliance with the dictates of the mental health industry; to 'take a knee' in solidarity with Black Lives Matter, but then turn a blind eye to the prison industrial complex that holds more African American slaves today than there ever were when slavery was acceptable in the US; to demand equal pay for the wealthiest women, but close your ears to the struggles of the poorest women whose plight demands major economic reform, all in accordance with the fundamentally inegalitarian ambitions of glass-ceiling feminism; to engage in self-righteous and destructive XR protests, without investing any emotional or intellectual intelligence in the choice of target. In multiple walks of life, it is always possible to wave a self-satisfying 'Not In My Name' flag, whilst your own hands are still covered in the shit you think you have cleaned off.

Are you an American citizen, for instance? Then you are personally responsible for every bomb that lands every 12 minutes, on countries with whom you are not at war. Yes, 'personally' because in a non-Cartesian democratic world, a human being is a person-in-community, not an individual-in-blissful-isolation. You may not approve, and you may not consent. But these actions are yours, personally. Again, we turn to the comedian, Lee Camp:

> 'While you get your gelato at the hip place where they put those cute little mint leaves on the side, someone is being bombed in your name. While you argue with the 17-year-old at the movie

> theatre who gave you a small popcorn when you paid for a large, someone is being obliterated in your name. While we sleep and eat and make love and shield our eyes on a sunny day, someone's home, family life, and body are being blown into a thousand pieces – in our names... Once every 12 minutes.' (Camp, *Bullet Points and Punchlines*, 2020, 58).

In a western democracy, whether I like it or not, whether I voted for them or not, the actions of my government are a representation of me. Saying that I 'voted for the other guy' does not absolve me of my government's crimes. I am still guilty by association. Their atrocities are committed in my name. I (and you, and they) are the *demos* of democracy, the 'people' who supposedly rule. And to think that listening to competing political parties, their promises and their mutual accusations, every few years before waddling into a cubicle to vote is the extent of my democratic responsibility, is to shower my shit-flakes on the great martyrs who secured our democratic rights. Democratic responsibility goes far beyond the voting booth, and further even than placard-waving protest. More often than not, to shout 'Not in my name' is just to echo Pontius Pilate's prophetic act and absolve myself of democratic responsibility.

This brings us all the way back to the trial of the lonely Jewish prophet, charged with undermining the status quo by speaking truth to power. Countless Christians accustomed to condemning Pilate for his guilty indifference, merrily repeat his actions when faced with similar situations today. Take the whistle-blower on trial for telling the truth about U.S. war crimes. According to the United Nations rapporteur on torture, these whistle-blowers are publicly defamed, humiliated, falsely accused, denied a fair trial, criminalised, tortured, and – if necessary – killed. All by our warm-hearted, fair-faced democratically elected western governments. All with my consent. In other words,

I. Am. Pilate.

And so are you. And our cherry-blossom-scented hands are still covered with putrid ass-wax.

CRUCIFIXION

Everyone knows that Jesus died. Poetic and over-familiar religious language can often shield the reader from grasping the simple tragedy of a life ending. Jesus did not merely 'call out' and 'breathe his last' or 'give up the ghost'. Rather, 'he shouted' and then 'he died'. A frightened and innocent young man, executed on a cross never intended for him, shouted and died. This was a micro example of the world's injustice, an injustice that remains intact in civilised western nations today. Innocent, powerless people lose. Powerful interests win. That is the message of the cross: Might is right.

> *When it was noon, darkness swept across the whole land until three in the afternoon. At three o'clock, Jesus shouted out with a loud voice, 'Eloi, Eloi, lema sabachthani?' which means, 'My God, my God, why have you abandoned me?' When some of the onlookers heard this, they said, 'Listen! He is calling for Elijah.' And someone ran, filled a sponge with sour wine, put it on a stick, and gave it to him to drink, saying, 'Wait! Let's see if Elijah will come and take him down.' Then Jesus gave a loud shout and died. And the curtain of the temple was torn in two, from top to bottom. Now, when the centurion who stood in front of him saw that this was how Jesus died, he said, 'In truth, this man was son of God.'*
> *(Mk 15:33-39)*

Socrates, whose death is perhaps the best attested in ancient history, almost seemed to enjoy his stoic departure from earth. Driven by a strange blend of arrogance and integrity, the philosopher courted his own fate, seemingly suffering a martyr complex of his own. Condemned to down a nice cup of hemlock, he finished his drink, and discoursed with his friends about the nature of his impending death. Unlike his companions, Socrates remained tearless and calm. His death could not be more dignified.

As shown above, Jesus was the very model of indignity. For one thing, he was shitting himself. There was no separation of body from soul here, no blessed release from his mortal frame. This young man was in anguish, not confident he could face the horrors that awaited him. And his physical suffering began even before his arrest. Knowing all that lay before him, he suffered a condition called hematohidrosis, a possible symptom of chronic fear as noted earlier. This occurs when tiny blood vessels constrict under stress, and then dilate and rupture. Blood seeps out through sweat glands. 'His sweat became like drops of blood.' (See section 4 above).

Within a matter of hours, he had been cross examined, mocked, publicly humiliated, beaten up, and subjected to a flogging. All that, before his crucifixion. If the more polite translations of the bible's original languages are correct, and this was the incident in which Jesus – apparently – 'breathed his last', there remains something of a question mark over which orifice he breathed it through. After all, the last breath of the human body is very often exhaled through the anus. This may well have been the case with Jesus. In fact, it is possible that the final bottom burp of a human life carries real substance. Here, it is worth contrasting the death bed scenes of other great figures of ancient history.

A contemporary of Jesus, the emperor Vespasian, died at a time when the 'imperial cult' (worship of the Roman Emperor) was gaining rapid prominence across the eastern realms of the empire. Once Vespasian realised his own end was nigh, he is reputed to have announced, 'Oh dear. I think I'm becoming a god.' Such a light-hearted and lofty epitaph was not attributed to less popular emperors.

Take Claudius, another contemporary. The Stoic philosopher Seneca offers this satirical account of the emperor's death:

> *At once he bubbled up the ghost, and there was an end to that shadow of a life... The last words he was heard to speak in this world were these. When he had made a great noise with that end of him which talked easiest, he cried out, 'Oh dear! I think I've shit myself.'* (Seneca, *Apocolocyntosis)*

People often shit themselves at the moment of death. It is only natural. Anyone who 'gives up the ghost' also gives up bowel control. Think of the implications for those Christians who like to wear a cross. Or perhaps, even more so, those who wear a crucifix (the symbol of the cross with the body of Jesus still nailed to it). Or think of all the artwork of the crucifixion that engages the senses. These artworks, this symbolism, these images, if they are to be fully authentic, must today include a faecal dimension. Those who wear the cross, ought really also to have a 'scratch-n-sniff' element to complete the symbolism. The cross stinks.

In all likelihood, the corpse of this Jewish dissident, hung on public display, was naked, bloodied and bruised, and stank of sweat and probably shit. Behold, the death of Jesus. This is a man totally robbed of dignity, devoid of justice and respect, penniless, homeless, friendless. Alone.

If today, you choose to wear a cross, you thereby choose to smear yourself with the very same shit. You declare to the world that you, you – the person right now with your heart beating and your lungs breathing – you, are willing to face that fate. As Terry Eagleton claims, 'If you follow Jesus, and don't end up dead, it appears you have some explaining to do' (Eagleton, *Reason, Faith and Revolution*, 2010, 46). The final execution of a frightened but subversive young man is often seen as an historical blip, the kind of thing that wouldn't happen in today's civilized society. But it was not some criminal thuggery that ended this innocent man's life. It was the most sophisticated legal system the world had seen.

Those who condemned Jesus were not horrible, evildoing nasties. They were good people. Civilized people. Sensible, rational, morally upright. There is nothing in today's world of peace-loving, rainbow flag-waving, convivial, sensible liberals that would give them any reason not to do exactly as the Romans did. We would crucify Jesus today. Why? Not because he was divine. But because he was so terrifyingly, disgustingly, excessively human. What made him so human was his intolerance for the bullshit I treasure. His very existence exposes me for who I am. And I don't want my delusions removed. When I consider myself the most liberal wokist – Jesus exposes my conscious ageism, my unselfconscious elitism, my utter tribalism, my indifference to economic injustice. When I consider myself a do-gooding, philanthropic Christian, he exposes how my true loyalties lie far from my stated loyalties, and how my true identity has nothing to do with the identity I claim for myself. When I consider myself indifferent to him, aloof and objective, he evokes my defensiveness: Jesus is the archetypal victim of my hidden privilege, of my passive complicity in the unjust order from which I benefit.

Legal institutions and political authorities in America, the United Kingdom, Australia and Sweden, all have recently proven their continuity with the politics that crucified Jesus. Again, we return to the fate of whistleblowers who have exposed imperial war crimes. These individuals are publicly vilified, falsely accused, mocked without consequence, and the voting populace is trained to hate them. Even the most intelligent and sophisticated media-consuming mobs have been trained to bay for the blood of those who expose the truth. There is no room in our happy order for those who threaten it.

Jesus of Nazareth was and is a threat to those who treasure order above all else. We have to get rid of him. And to let the world see what happens to those who question the order we treasure. In this light, the cross of Jesus exposes how the ruling order, the social, political, economic order – fair-faced and charming and rational – functions as an unstoppable, implacable death machine. Throughout his life, and especially in the moment of his death, Jesus represents those who are the victims of justice and goodness and rationality, as those qualities are embodied by the ruling order. He represents the shit of the earth. And in all likelihood, his final act was an involuntary public shit as he hung on the cross. Stain your glass with that image! Jesus loved you so much, he shat himself for you.

RESURRECTION

High mortality rates and short life expectancy. Those peasants who saw out their lives in the occupied territories of a brutal imperial regime knew the face of death. People died. Not in a hospital, hospice, or retirement home. But right under your nose. Dead bodies. Visible and, if you leave them too long, smellable. And when corpses are the product of crucifixion at the hands of experienced executioners, they do not make a glorious return to mortality. So, when Jesus' body goes missing, and a young stranger is offering cryptic advice and issuing strange commands, the response of three women is bowel-watering fear. This is how the earliest known version of Mark's Gospel ends. Fear.

When the Sabbath was over, Mary Magdalene, and Mary the mother of James, and Salome, bought spices in order to go and anoint Him. Very early on the first day of the week, they came to the tomb after sunrise. They were saying to one another, 'Who will roll the stone from the entrance of the tomb for us?'

Looking up, they saw the stone had been rolled away, although it was extremely big. On entering the tomb, they saw a young man sitting at the right, wearing a white robe, and they were gob smacked.

He said to them, 'Don't look so surprised! You are looking for Jesus of Nazareth, who has been crucified. He has got up. He is not here. Look! Here is the place where they laid him. But go and tell his disciples and Peter, "He is going ahead of you to Galilee. You will see him there, just as He told you."'

They went out and fled from the tomb, because shock and awe had gripped them. They said nothing to anyone because they were afraid. (Mark 16:1-8)

My least glorious moment in the British military occurred whilst serving as a 'Car-Door-Opener' for a VIP visit. As I recall, he was a cousin of the then Queen. Car-Door-Opening was no easy task. There are multiple considerations to take into account: a constant scan of the surrounding buildings for potential protestors or assassins; a particular place to stand in order to ease transition from the vehicle; an agreed set of words suitable for addressing a dignitary; and a particular manner in which the car door is subsequently closed. Not to mention, dressing in your very best 'Number One' uniform, a military attire reserved for ceremonial parades. Wearing such a uniform required hours of preparation in pressing shirt, trousers and jacket, polishing buttons and badges, and shining shoes. I was spotless, immaculate. But this only added to the anxiety I felt at the occasion.

Thankfully, I had been carefully trained in the art of car-door-opening, and I was ready.

As the black Bentley rolled into view, however, I noted a growing dot in the sky. Heading straight for me, it closed in at an alarming rate and seemed destined to arrive at the same nanosecond as the Bentley. Despite being forty miles from the coast, the dot was a seagull. A seagull with a gut disorder. An avian weapons platform bearing such a heavy payload I am astonished it was able to part company with *terra firma* in the first place. Worse still, this was a seagull with an astonishing degree of precision. Needless to say, as I opened the car door… PHHHUTT! A small tin of grey paint landed on me from the heavens and decorated my Number One uniform. I was covered in shit.

The VIP stood back for a second, inspected the state of my uniform, worked out what had happened and burst into laughter. Some dignitary. He laughed all the way along the path and into the Station Headquarters. Once he and his hosts were out of earshot, my sergeant leaned over and whispered, 'Should have worn your *Number Two* Uniform.'

'Oi you!' The Warrant Officer's distant, angry voice bellowing at me. This man terrified my twenty-year-old self. 'Get your soiled arse over here now.' I was summoned to the Station Guardroom. 'Why,' he said, trying not to laugh. 'Why does it always happen to you?' He threatened to make me mow the grass on the airfield using a pair of nail clippers, and assured me this was the last time I would be entrusted with such a prestigious role.

Reflecting on the pristine state of my Number One uniform, it is difficult not to recall again Saint Paul's phrase concerning his own spotless righteousness. He was, after all, not just a religious zealot, but a radical law-abiding example of Pharisaic purity and perfection. And, in light of his encounter with the heavenly righteousness of Christ, he looked at his religious observances and concluded, 'I consider them shit.' (Phil. 3:8).

But just how righteous is the heavenly Father who, in order to maintain his own immaculate image, had his son tortured and killed?

Christians and atheists alike have often viewed the events surrounding the death and resurrection of Jesus as an act of divine child abuse. A strict father punishing his innocent offspring. Christians often try to justify this, by declaring – oh, it's okay, because God raised him from the dead right afterwards, so we can all live happily ever after. And hey presto, the image of a pure, spotless Jesus, sacrificed on behalf of a guilt-ridden humanity.

Historically, the picture is likely to have been very different.

There was nothing attractive, pure or innocent about the failed Messiah nailed to a torture device outside the gates of Jerusalem. To the political establishment, he was a barbarian, a pain-in-the-arse outsider, a trouble-making terrorist. As a threat to political authority, he was crucified outside the walls of the *polis,* the civilised precincts of the state. Outside, where all refuse and filth belong. There is nothing attractive about crucified criminals – not least because they have likely shit themselves. (Having examined photographs of its entire length, I am pretty sure there are skid-marks on the Turin shroud.) Nothing attractive, nothing spotless about the man who epitomises the 'the scum of the earth'. In its origins, that phrase itself is a biblical description of the folk Jesus represented, the church (I Cor 4:13), though a poor translation of the original Greek.

The Marxist literary critic, Terry Eagleton, has a far more authentic translation for this phrase. He understood well enough that the solidarity encouraged and embodied by Jesus of Nazareth shows a picture of a loving god and a Christian church that are wildly at odds with most modern conceptions.

> The only authentic image of this violently loving God is a tortured and executed political criminal, who dies in an act of solidarity with what the Bible calls the anawim, meaning the destitute and dispossessed. Crucifixion was reserved by the Romans for political offences alone. The anawim, in [Saint Paul's] phrase, are the shit of the earth – the scum and refuse of society who constitute the cornerstone of the new form of human life known as the kingdom of God. Jesus himself is consistently presented as their representative. (Eagleton, *Reason, Faith and Revolution*, 2010, 23)

Jesus is not ceremoniously displayed in a clean white night dress, an image of the sacrificial dove or the unblemished lamb. If there is innocence in this political criminal on the cross, it is the innocence of the disgusting outsider, the threat, the recipient of legitimate violence in the view of the majority. This is not divine child abuse. This is human violence. This is the holy father, the Roman emperor, imposing his violence on those whose presence is a threat to his order. The death of Jesus is not some terrible extra-judicial lynching conducted by a mindless mob. Jesus was condemned by the very best legal system that the civilised world had to offer, with the complicity of the most complex religious system in the empire. To those who wield power (and despite Pilate's apparent protest), the death of Jesus was just and right and sensible and fair. The kingdom of God was defeated. Jesus was a shit, and his followers – the shit of the earth – were revealed as such at Calvary.

And then his body goes missing.

If the resurrection was an actual, historical event, it represents a radically alternative version of power at work in the world. This is not the almighty power (omni-potence) associated with Roman emperors. This is a totally different kind of power. Not a power that will reveal itself on the battlefields of the mighty, nor in the bank accounts of the oligarchs, nor in the public image of the celebrity. As Eagleton concludes,

> Power is now, in principle, in the hands of those whom it has traditionally spurned as so much refuse and garbage. If the founding act of civilisation now involves a gesture of exclusion [a human sacrifice conducted beyond the city gates], this new regime reverses that repression, as the slab rejected by the builders becomes the cornerstone of a new dispensation (Eagleton, *Radical Sacrifice*, 2018, 27).

In other words, to the political establishment, Jesus is the turd that won't flush. And in his wake, his devotees constitute the sewage that bubbles up into the street. The challenge of the resurrection is issued, first and foremost, to a political and economic status quo, and those who support it. Jesus and his followers ruin the orderliness of unjust systems of power.

For most of us, when we read about heroes and villains, we naturally assume that we would occupy the position of the story's hero. We are nothing like the establishment figures that would crucify an innocent Jesus with his sad eyes and his pure white nighty. But the actual sacrifice of the historical Jesus is nothing so Hollywood. Jesus is a threat to be silenced and swept under the carpet in order to maintain our own clean self-image. And our self-image is clearly not that of an oppressive regime. After all, we opposed Donald Trump and waved a 'resistance' banner. Surely, oppression is what happens under a swastika but never under a rainbow flag. We care about diversity and equality and inclusivity. How could we possibly be in the wrong? Innocent. Woke. Pure. We wear a Number One uniform.

Oblivious to our own selective solidarity, the limits on our diversity, and the blind-spots of our inclusivity, we may well treasure a delusional self-image. It is perfectly possible that, despite such high-sounding virtues, we would still exclude and persecute a figure as troublesome as Jesus of Nazareth. Republican and Democrat, Conservative and Labour, Royalist and Revolutionary, when we unconsciously revel in our collective self-righteousness, we may miss that tiny dot in the sky.

And the dot is growing.

That is the promise of the resurrection.

VI

Concluding Reflections

THE BLASPHEMY OF FARTLESSNESS

To claim that Jesus farted, or to focus on divine faecal matter will no doubt sound blasphemous to modern Christians whose identity has been shaped more by secular culture than by Holy Scripture. Many will at least question the morality of highlighting the importance of shitting and farting in relation to Jesus of Nazareth. Affirming that a human Jesus must have 'gone to the toilet' is one thing. This book-length preoccupation with the toiletry dimensions of his humanity is something else, perhaps bordering on the obscene. As Christians, after all, you're not supposed to be rude, or crude, or dishonourable. What is more, when your crudity is directed at no less than God himself, then surely you are in the realm of blasphemy.

In an era when digital voices have multiplied beyond number and those left clamouring for attention resorting to ever cruder, more shocking and more scatological language, it sounds like a fair question. Nowadays, everyone's an amateur journalist with internet access. Those working in the media confirm that headlines filling the newspapers, airwaves, twitter-feeds and digital timelines are becoming noticeably more extreme in their use of language. Journalists themselves are forced to play along with increasing the shock-factor of their tag-lines in a desperate bid to ensure their voices are heard against millions of competitors. By drawing attention to the basest, crudest aspects of Jesus's life, am I not simply dragging God's name through excrement in search of clicks? The answer is that I don't have to drag God's name through the shit. God's name is already in the shit because that's where his people are. And if it Isn't, then it's where they should be.

The point is perhaps best illustrated by relaying a shit-related incident. Having worked as a senior member of a beautiful Oxford college, I had the privilege of booking guest-rooms for visiting family and friends at a very reasonable rate. One Monday morning, however, I was summoned by college staff members to behold the room where one of my guests had stayed over the weekend. On my arrival the door opened, and I was instantly hit by a tidal wave of malodorous vapour. On inquiring as to the nature of the atrocity committed herein, I learned from a half-asphyxiated voice spluttering through a handkerchief, that my guest had defecated on the carpet. I quickly scanned this immaculate apartment in search of the evidence, anything large enough to inflict such an omnipotent degree of nasal terror, but I could see nothing obvious. Naturally, I volunteered to begin the clean-up. It was then I learned not only that the valiant professional clean-up was already complete, but that prior to this my guest had also removed the turd and attempted to clean up after him/herself. Apparently, it is extremely difficult to clean up after shit. And this was just one sole human turd, deposited and then disposed of several hours earlier. Still the mere trace of its pollutants created a 'forced air environment' with rancid toxicity of supernatural magnitude. And another guest was soon due to arrive.

Now picture the new guest arriving, taking one whiff of the malicious vapours, exhibiting a gag-reflex and retreating as rapidly as possible towards fresh air. That is precisely the action of the cartesian Christ, the holy Jesus who inhabits a realm other than the realm of mortals, the pseudo-saviour who is so heavenly minded he is of no earthly use. This is the Holman Hunt portrayal of a modern Christ who softly whispers, 'Behold I stand at the door and knock' (Rev 3:20), but when the door is opened and the odours hit, suddenly remembers he has a subsequent engagement. This, in sum, is the systemic blasphemy woven through the creed of modern Christianity.

The overwhelmingly dominant Christian belief in a shit-less God and a fart-less Jesus is in urgent need of correction. That is, the blasphemous belief in a God who refuses to dirty his hands with human shit and a Jesus who is not really human after all. Cartesian Christians worship a God who – for the sake of pristine holiness – retreats from the genuinely terrible things that happen in the world. It is hardly surprising that worshippers of this excretaphobic idol hear him declare, 'Go thou and do likewise'. This is the Christian reality that – a generation ago – famously led sociologist Tony Campolo to unburden himself on a Christian platform, by declaring,

> I have three things I'd like to say today. First, while you were sleeping last night, 30,000 kids died of starvation or diseases related to malnutrition. Second, most of you don't give a shit. What's worse is that you're more upset with the fact that I said shit than the fact that 30,000 kids died last night. (Tony Campolo)

Those kids and their families were drowning in shit. But the Cartesian Christ – who remains the reigning idol of modern Christian religion – has no business venturing into the stinking horror in which so many real people are submerged. It is enough for him to attend to the privatised individual wellbeing of those deluded enough to worship him. This is the God who has turned his back on humanity (unless you belong to a highly if unwittingly privileged segment of our species). It is also the God whom Friedrich Nietzsche pronounced dead, Bertrand Russell declared immoral, Christopher Hitchens denounced as evil, and whose tired and fetid corpse Pat Robertson is still wheeling around trying to pass-off as worthy of adoration and praise.

A radically different portrait of God is found in both Jewish and Christian scriptures. The God of these ancient texts is far more submerged in the gritty, horrible realities that humans face. Nor does he wield omnipotent power, omnipotence being the attribute of Greek and Roman emperors and gods.

Though Israel's God sits on a throne, this is not a God seated on high, removed from the grovelling, snivelling unpersons whose compliance he demands. This idea of an aloof God is rooted in the classical Olympian deities. The gods of Mount Olympus are the sociopathic family who live on a diet of tinned rice pudding and divinely supercharged Red Bull and – not surprisingly – are cursed with (literally) titanic anger management issues.

Obsessed with their own wellbeing and the worship due to them, they are not remotely interested in the struggles of mortals (unless you belong to that tiny slither of the population called 'heroes'). To be on the radar of the Greek gods, you have to be good-looking, upright and virtuous, noble, wealthy and powerful. Belief in the God of Christianity and Judaism is often shoe-horned into this ancient conception of divinity. Gods who – like the targets of Campolo's invective – couldn't give a shit about human suffering.

The God of Scripture is viscerally affected by the plight of people who suffer, and takes human form in the midst of it. His attention is directed not towards those who are fine, happy and comfortable, but to those who find themselves in the shit and who know that's where they are. God's attention is not aimed at the delusional, perfected fantasies of the human self or the human world in all its fake innocence and manufactured happiness. The God of Scripture directs his attention towards those facing up to the lies about themselves, the fantasies they inhabit, at those addressing the most putrid components of their own personhood and the world as it really is. This is not the Jesus who knocks on the door only to offer a gag-reflex at the stink of excrement from within. He is not repulsed by it, because he has lived with it and in it. This is the Jesus who was already there on his hands and knees, washing human faeces out of the carpet. Since the New Testament portrays Jesus as 'the image of the invisible God' (Col 1:15), then he is a shit-scrubbing saviour. To portray him otherwise is blasphemy.

VULGARITY AND APOSTASY

Whilst it may be possible to accept that Jesus did indeed relieve his bladder, empty his bowels and vent his intestinal gasses – is it really necessary to use vulgar language to communicate the theological implications of this? If it is possible to communicate in inoffensive language that lacks vulgarity, why revert to crude Anglo Saxon swear-words? Is this not a vain attempt to be needlessly provocative? Especially when the New Testament prohibits '*obscenity, foolish talk or coarse joking*' (Eph 5:4, NIV). These seemingly pious words were written in a letter (often attributed to the Christian apostle, Saint Paul) to the Christian community in the ancient city of Ephesus.

> *But immorality or any impurity or greed must not even be named among you, as is proper among saints; and there must be* ***no filthiness*** *and* ***silly talk****, or* ***coarse jesting****, which are not fitting, but rather giving of thanks. For this you know with certainty, that no immoral or impure person or covetous man, who is an idolater, has an inheritance in the kingdom of Christ and God.*
> *(Eph 5:3-5, NASB)*

This – like most modern translations of the verses – is misleading. The author's prohibitions are presented as depressing cultural conformity with a religious mindset devoid of fun, laughter and conversation. A far better translation is to read these instructions to a young Christian community as radically counter-cultural. Throughout the Roman world, there were no job references or official qualifications, so your reputation or 'honour' was crucial to your wellbeing. You advanced through life by seeking to gain honour and avoid shame. In a society dominated by honour/shame hierarchies, the Ephesian Christians are exhorted to refrain altogether from engaging in the gossip-dynamics essential to a shame culture (i.e., to refrain from shameful talk – usually translated *'obscenity'* or *'filthiness'*).

Secondly, *'foolish talk'* or *'silly talk'* is not simply joining in with the coarse conversations of idiots. It is better understood as a preoccupation with trivia, passing itself off as well-informed and serious. The modern-day equivalent is having your beliefs shaped by the echo-chamber of your Facebook timeline or Twitter feed, or even earnest conversations about 'the news' (or what the corporate media dictates is newsworthy). This is not merely 'silly' (NRSV) since *'foolish talk'* can be profoundly intelligent and well informed.

Thirdly, *'coarse joking'* or *'vulgar talk'* (NRSV), refers really to the 'clever wit' that thrives on the gossip and triviality that characterise the first two prohibitions. In cultural interactions, being quick-witted would gain honour for you and shame for anyone you 'take down' or joke about.

Taken together, Paul's condemnation of *'obscenity, foolish talk or coarse joking'* converges perfectly with the philosopher Martin Heidegger's threefold exasperation with 'the They-self'. That is, a way of being that has unwittingly surrendered to some kind of mass-produced, inauthentic way of living – a world that processes humans through life like sausages through a factory production-line. Regardless of whether the sausages were educated at Eton or Harvard, regardless of whether they vote Republican or Democrat, and regardless of whether they are Atheist or Christian, the sausages usually regard themselves as 'free-thinkers'. However, by engaging in the three kinds of talk Heidegger describes as *curiosity, ambiguity* and *idle-talk* they reveal their status as social, intellectual and moral herd animals. These three practices correspond perfectly with the kind of talk Saint Paul sought to prohibit. His prohibition had nothing and absolutely nothing to do with forbidding Christians from using vulgar language. After all, Paul himself was happy to use such language (Phil 3:8; I Cor 4:13; cf Gal 5:12). But if – according to Scripture – Christians have the *right* to use vulgarity, does that mean they have the *duty*? Instead of using potentially offensive language about pissing, shitting and farting – would it not be more sensitive to use bigger words derived from Latin: urination, defecation, flatulation? After all, both sets of words refer to the same things. However, although both sets of words *denote* the same objects, the monosyllables also *connote* far broader categories of crudeness. That is, shit, piss and fart have *connotations* of insult, rudeness, unthinking profanity, usually because these words are frequently used by the uneducated, unreflective, unenlightened and uncouth semi-illiterate masses.

It was for those ignorant masses that Thomas Wycliffe translated the Bible into English in the Fourteenth Century. The reaction of Church authorities is encapsulated in a statement published in 1395.

> This pestilent and wretched John Wycliffe, that son of the old serpent..., translated from Latin into English the Gospel, [indeed all of the Scriptures,] that Christ gave to the clergy and doctors of the Church. So that by his means it has become vulgar and more open to laymen and women who can read than it usually is to quite learned clergy of good intelligence. And so the pearl of the Gospel, [indeed of the Scriptures in toto,] is scattered abroad and trodden underfoot by swine.
>
> (*Church Chronicle*)

Wycliffe was accused of 'vulgarity' not because his translation of the Holy Bible makes generous use of such fine English words as bollocks, turds and piss. These were not considered obscenities in the Fourteenth Century. Vulgar here, really meant common, popular, widely available, comprehensible by the masses – it was the language of the portacabin. Vulgarity is considered negatively only by those keen to distinguish themselves from their inferiors – those who are too good for the world of the portacabin.

In her magnificent study, *Holy Shit,* Melissa Mohr traces the history of vulgarity. The strands of that history are complex and my brief summary does no justice to her lively and fascinating account. In sum, she highlights how what constitutes 'crudity' and 'vulgarity' changes over time. In a feudal culture dominated by Christianised hierarchy and in which honour and shame were key dynamics, 'swearing' referred to swearing oaths as evidence of a person's credibility. To swear falsely or unthinkingly was an offence to God himself and the entire social hierarchy on which he was perched. By contrast common words like shit, piss and fart (along with a host of others) were not deemed rude, nor crude, nor coarse. They were simply direct, functional descriptions for natural elements of everyday life.

As the feudal society gave way to the capitalist and Christendom gave way to Secularism, the notion of obscenity shifted radically. In the feudal era, one's place in the social hierarchy was obvious and inescapable (royalty, nobility, priests, artisans and peasants). In the capitalist era, however, it was far less so. Social boundaries became fluid as people acquired (or lost) wealth. Here, speech became far more important as an indicator of one's place in the social hierarchy. If you wanted to be perceived as a worthy, respectable individual then you needed more than money. You also had to distinguish yourself as far as possible from those who were 'vulgar' – i.e., common, widespread, the popular majority of human beings – in effect, your inferiors.

Crudely put, the implications of this – from a biblical perspective – are that taking offence at crude language rests ultimately on seeking to secure your place over against your social inferiors. Those at the top with no need to secure their place, may continue to 'swear like a Lord.' Those at the bottom, with no hope of climbing the social ladder may as well 'swear like a navvy.' But for the rest, the cultural game was clear. The fact that all manner of social rules and moral sensibilities have built up around this tendency does complicate it. We may feel offence at vulgarity through no fault of our own, because our social context has formed and trained us to feel offended. But let us be clear. The righteous offence we may feel is certainly not based on any biblical teaching. It arises from confinement within what Heidegger called 'the They-self'. Preoccupation with what They say, what They will think. It is perfectly possible, after all, to refrain from 'filthiness', 'silly talk' and 'coarse jesting' and by so doing trap ourselves inside the godless ideological echo chamber of the They-self. Equally possible is for those from the world of the portacabin, where foul-mouthed profanities come as naturally as breathing, to enjoy the genuinely 'authentic' existence of those liberated from the They-self.

This book is an interpretation of the Gospels. The language in which they are penned is vulgar (or *koine*, in Greek). Most of the people it features are vulgar. The events narrated took place among an underclass of nobodies who threatened the unassailable might of the They-self: the brutal rule of a pagan empire; the financial interests of distant overlords and their local sock-puppets; the religious ideologies that demanded either rebellion or submission. The authors of the Gospels and the earliest Christians had no influence in society. They hailed from the portacabin rather than the palace. History may well have waved its wand and turned them into 'great men', but they were vulgar. To deny them their true, authentic vulgarity is apostasy – the abandonment of the true faith.

THE LIBERATION OF FLATULENCE

Major casinos are carefully designed to create a timeless, space-less environment. There are no clocks to remind you of real time. There are no windows to remind you of your real location. There are no boundaries, no corners on carpets, no clear transitions from one area to another – because crossing these boundaries can jolt the minds of gamblers out of their mesmerised state and bring them back to their bodily senses. The layout of the casino is designed to keep customers at the slot machines, dislocated from time and space, forgetful of the physical world outside, temporarily ignorant of the real-world consequences of their present actions.

Modern Christianity as a religion is largely designed in the same way as the casino, creating a timeless, space-less fantasy Jesus to replace the dangerously explosive biblical Jesus. The Jesus of the Bible was politically dangerous to the empire because he sought to instigate regime change (by heralding the Kingdom of God). He was economically dangerous because he promoted debt cancellation (in a world that required debts to be honoured). He was socially dangerous because he sought to displace one worldview with another (an all-encompassing paradigm shift).

Christianity re-cast this Jesus as a docile do-gooder who was no real danger to anyone. It turned the Kingdom of God (socially just rule in the present) into a place called *heaven* – the final resting place of the tediously well-behaved. It turned the cancellation of debt (a major economic reform) into the *forgiveness of sins* – wiping clean your moral slate before a supernatural mind-reading judge. It turned the process of changing one's entire worldview (a painful if liberating exercise) into the submissive act of *repentance* (apologising to God on a daily basis for being born a mere human.)

Where the earliest followers of Christ were a threat to the smooth running of the empire, Christianity sank a political tranquilliser into this dangerous movement – entrancing the faithful with the portrait of a timeless moral guru, preoccupied with future bliss and treating the present world as an uncomfortable waiting room for the afterlife. The Church of Christendom became the Taj Mahal casino of Trump – disconnected from the gritty reality of an outside world, keeping worshippers sedated, protecting them from the slightest cause to question their confinement, lest they stop feeding the insatiable machinery of cash-collection. The mesmerised casino-Christians of the modern era are perfectly content to remain confined 'in the zone' as gamblers call it, inside that unquestioning state of blissful dystopia in which even a great win is an unwelcome interruption.

How can the stupefied subordinates of this collective delusion be disabused of their timeless beliefs and break free from the They-self? How is it possible to uproot precious convictions that have sunk their roots so deeply into the modern psyche? This book is an exhortation that modern readers cup their ears towards history, to hear the flatulence of Jesus rumble in the distance. In this light, the farting of Christ might save the world. A messianic bowel eruption is a liberating event. A liberationist burble from the hind quarters of the historical Jesus may, after all, be the only force that compels gamblers to flee the Christianised casino fantasy in search of fresh air.

I can already hear Biblical scholars tearing out their otic hairs in anger - that this approach commits 'eisegesis', that is – the practice of imposing onto the text an idea that cannot be found in the text itself. And sure enough, there are no farts in the Bible. However, a far worse case of 'eisegesis' is to impose onto the interpretation of scripture the alien belief that Jesus did not fart. As mentioned from the outset, the view of a non-physical Jesus is a heresy called 'Docetism'. It portrays a spiritual, disembodied, and therefore disembowelled figure – implausible and unhistorical. To focus on flatulence is to pay heed to the basest, lowest, simplest of human expression – to allow it to ripple through our assumptions about this Jesus to re-conceive his sheer humanity from the bottom up.

Although each section of the book has focussed on one specific incident narrated in the Gospels, it does not hear farts where there are none. Instead, it is an attempt to open up avenues of historical insight that have long remained morally barred by those who have raised themselves above all vulgarity. The interpretations offered above are from and for the portacabin – a haven of intelligence and ignorance, of odour and warmth, friendship and ridicule, and of course, vulgarity.

There are truths about the historical Jesus immediately obvious to portacabin regulars that would remain out of bounds for those more accustomed to the pristine environments of the church and the university. And it is those vulgar truths that need to be heard. After all, when history is heard well, it is also smelt and felt. But these and other dimensions of history are simply not on the radar of most professional historians, biblical historians included. What Cornell West terms the 'deodorised discourse' of modernity has produced a sanitized Christ detached from his vulgar context, his vulgar followers and his vulgar claims.

In order to find an alternative, the interpretations offered above rest on a series of vulgar stories that some will consider amusing. For many, farting is inexplicably hilarious – presumably because it crashes suddenly and unexpectedly through all manner of social barriers. In the portacabin farts are rarely funny, because they are not prohibited. Anyone who 'uncorks a jeroboam' into a portacabin will not raise an eyebrow – assuming the fumes are odourless. No social boundaries are transgressed, and no one present is either shocked or amused. In the senior common room of an ancient university however – where civilized and educated intellectuals partake in sophisticated discourse – unrestrained bodily eruptions defy all manner of social taboos. When a professor accidentally punctuates the conversation with an unpremeditated rectal squelch, it is difficult to keep a straight face. Similarly, in a church, during the silence after the confession for instance, high-volume, hi-octane anal bellowing leaves even the most faithful worshipper convulsing with restrained hysteria. On one occasion, the walloping guff issued by one pious back-pipe was so strange it was mistaken for a voice. (Apostates would have described it as 'farting in tongues'). People laugh at farts because flatulential outbursts penetrate uncrossable barriers and break social taboos, uniting the vulgar and the privileged on the level plain of base, bodily human life.

When I once had the privilege of quizzing the brilliant Miriam Margolyes about farting, her principal observation was that it promotes not only laughter but unity:

> ...
>
> *Miriam: If I want to break wind, I am going to break wind... I always give advanced warning. I always say, 'I am going to fart'. And then I fart... I think it's just human. And when I fart, I notice that people laugh. And that's lovely isn't it? It's a wonderful thing if you can make people laugh. I think that [farting] brings people together and makes them feel relaxed.*
>
> *Perry: It does grease the wheels of human interaction...*
>
> *Miriam: I hope not 'grease'.*

Margolyes' insight highlights the necessity of flatulence-appreciation in a world that is socially disintegrating into separate interest groups. That disintegration is largely invisible to us: the emergence of 'identity politics' (where the only good people are those who share my very particular concerns); the 'us vs them' mentality (cultivated by a media industry whose sophisticated consumers are trained not to hear the other side); the construction of 'echo-chambers' (inhabited by intelligent people who are convinced they are well-informed and circumspect); the social-media networks (where my unselfconsciously manufactured gullibility becomes a saleable commodity). The overall effect is to reduce the human beings who exist beyond the boundaries of my mass-produced but oh-so-personal concerns are reduced to what George Orwell described as 'unpersons.'

Jesus of Nazareth is, and always has been, an 'unperson' in this sense. That is, one of those real human beings in the real world whose dangerous voices are quietly erased and whose true legacies are airbrushed out of history. The very real boundaries that separate 'us' from 'them' and leave us oblivious to the voice of the 'other', are thus rendered invisible to us. Unpersons are quietly banished from the realm of our concern. Alternatives no longer exist. And hey presto. It is not only Christians trapped in the ideological casino. The modern world is designed like Trump's Taj Mahal, with all transition points smoothed over, where social boundaries are rounded out, camouflaged, disguised – just in case addicts are jolted momentarily back into reality. The antidote? The way out, the exodus, the salvation from this hopeless matrix-existence? God-given holy flatulence. It transgresses boundaries to which we were oblivious. It highlights our common humanity. It brings people together. In a world advancing towards disintegration, the peace-making humanoid arse-blast may reconcile Christians with Christ, the self with the other, the body with the mind. Thank God for the simple human fart, a veritable miracle of nature.

THE END

Gratitude

The writing of this book was fuelled entirely by the friendliness and the caffeine of staff at Maison Clement Bakery, Newnham- namely, Leo Irvin and Alise Solovjova, Charlotte Lee and Sam Faghy, Sebastien Giraldo and others. These fine folk worked the early morning shifts and offered the animated opinion as well as the artisan coffee that motivated the 7-8am writing of each chapter.

Books like this are the fruit of collaboration, and I wish I could thank everyone who – over the years – has unknowingly provided material for the more vulgar elements of this book. I would like to thank those who have heard and interacted with early versions in seminars, conversations and other talks, in particular, members of Cambridge University's Student Christian Movement, and for students and staff from the Philology Department of the University of Rzeszow. In particular, I remain very grateful to the brilliant Dr Patrycja Austin for the insight, critique and encouragement she offered for each chapter.

Several students at Robinson College, Cambridge have been of enormous help, especially members of our boxing club: Ilana Cope, Jumeira Nathan, Charlotte Duckett and Tamsin Sandhu. The insights of Max Mason, Zafirah Badmus, and Dylan Stewart have always been lively and helpful. Then three magnificently rogue Theologians, Anna Zvolikevych, Ella Jones and Lili Cooper, as well as Ben Cole and other members of Robinson Chapel Choir.

Above all, thank you to the narrator of the audiobook, Dr Tim Atkin, whose appreciation of *Jesus Farted* and his ability to bring the text to life, has added real substance to my venting.

Printed in Great Britain
by Amazon